HEALING A BROKEN HEART

Part I

Annette Carnes

Healing a Broken Heart

Cover Design by Istvan Szabo, Ifj.

Ararity Press Publications
Contact Jeri Darby @ araritypress@gmail.com
Jeri Darby / Facebook
989 717-1031

HEALING A BROKEN HEART

Part I

Only Jesus Can Heal a Broken Heart and Make Us New…

ANNETTE CARNES

TABLE OF CONTENTS

Dedication.......................................7
Acknowledgement.......................................9
Foreword.......................................10
Introduction.......................................11
CHAPTER ONE: Healing a Broken Heart.......................................13
Faith to Step Out.......................................19
Aligned with God.......................................23
The Light of the World.......................................26
CHAPTER TWO: God's Love Casts Out Fear.......................................31
Look and Live!.......................................40
CHAPTER THREE: Fruit of the Spirit.......................................53
The Power of God's Compassion.......................................54
Jesus Will Never Leave Us.......................................57
A Call to Witness.......................................58
CHAPTER FOUR: The Path of Life.......................................68
Kidnapped!.......................................71
The Wrong Mentality.......................................75
Hurting People Hurt People.......................................76
He Heals the Wounded Heart.......................................79
Healing a Wounded Soul.......................................83
Words are Powerful!.......................................85
The Power of thoughts and Words.......................................86
CHAPTER FIVE: How About Your Heart?.......................................90
Forgive Them From Your Heart.......................................94
Speak Words of Life.......................................97
Chapter Six: We Are In a Battle.......................................101
Choose to Accept the Assignment!.......................................105
Stand!.......................................108
Stand for Others.......................................112

DEDICATION

So many wonderful friends and ministers have helped me and encouraged me to write this book. I can only mention a few for the sake of space. My children Candy, Lori, John and Kendra my daughter-in-love came to my rescue numerous times when my computers went haywire. Writing the book was easy because the Spirit of the Lord flowed right through me. It was my computer that went crazy, wiping out entire chapters, freezing so I could not retrieve materials and dying before my book was complete. A friend gave me two computers that I had to rig together to get one to function. The first time I bought them to meet with my publisher they malfunctioned. Finally, she said, "Get them out of my sight!" We both struggled not to laugh.

I said, "Maybe I better break down and buy a new one."

Jeri said, "What was your first clue?" We both burst into laughter.

My sister Joan said my "book is anointed by the Holy Spirit." This encouraged me to not give up and throw it away.

Pastors James and Leona Glenn helped me to believe that God would enable me to complete my book and said, "fear not." My publisher, Jeri Darby with Ararity Press Publications was patient and reassured me that publishing my book was easy; because "I am a good writer." This book has only been possible by the help of the Lord. He did the work in me and through me. I pray that this book will help my readers identify the broken places in their hearts so they can bring them to the Lord for healing.

ACKNOWLEDGEMENT

Apostle James Glenn
Pastor of Center of Attraction
Saginaw MI

Annette Carnes has with purpose, precision and tender care ministered the gospel of Christ to multitudes. I can say this because I've seen her in action for years at TCT (Tri-State Christian Television), with her smile and sweet demeanor, she truly demonstrated in person and on the prayer lines the love of Christ. Many lives were changed because of Annette.

Annette is truly a minister on a mission to save the lost and heal the broken hearted. There is no one else I can think of who has the biblical know-how and life experience to write this book "Healing a Broken Heart."

Jesus said, in this world you will have tribulation (pain, sorrow, trouble) but be of good cheer for I have overcome the world. Annette, in her book will show you how Jesus can heal you of a broken heart and overcome life's troubles by God's word. This book is a must read for every person.

FOREWORD

Eunice Good
Restoring Father's Heart Ministry

I have had the privilege of learning to know Annette Carnes through being members of the same church, prayer times together and her participation in classes that I have taught. She is truly an amazing prayer warrior, a passionate lover of God and is consumed by God's presence while declaring His love and goodness in the earth.

Annette Carnes takes the reader through her live adventures portraying her pathway to wholeness of experiential comprehension and understanding of God's faithfulness and great love. Her gentle spirit and compassionate heart for people rings true throughout this book.

She clearly expresses how God uses life experiences to develop His fruit of the Spirit in people's lives so each can become more like Him. Her key to being strong and effective in her sphere of influence is dedicating time in the secret place of the Most High, delighting, communing and worshipping in Father's intimate presence. Her greatest desire is to bring people to God for cleansing, healing, restoration and transformation.

It's my pleasure and delight to commend you to the life, ministry and the writings of one of God's faithful prayer warrior's. Listen to her plea. Annette Carnes will help you find your steps to freedom, healing and restoration for your life to be filled with God's power and compassionate love for others. Do you want God's freedom, healing, power and compassion? Then read on!

INTRODUCTION

The Lord told a well-known and powerful minister one day as he was praying, that there is something terrible on earth that we hardly even notice, but is echoed all over heaven with great emotion. That terrible thing is a broken heart in one of His beloved children. If Jesus cares so much for our broken hearts, you can be sure He has an answer and healing all planned out for us. Jesus knows our pain, not only because He knows our thoughts and emotions as God, but also because He experienced it when He was on earth. Isaiah was speaking of Jesus when he wrote the following verses:

> ***Who has believed our report? And to whom has the arm of the Lord (Jesus is referred to as Father God's arm) been revealed?***
>
> ***For He shall grow up before Him as a tender plant and as a root out of dry ground. He has no form or comeliness; and when we see Him, there is no beauty that we should desire Him.***
>
> ***He is despised and rejected by men, a man of sorrows and acquainted with grief. And we hid, as it were, our faces from Him. He was despised, and we did not esteem Him.***
> ***Surely, He has borne our griefs and carried our sorrows, yet we esteemed Him stricken, smitten by God, and afflicted.***
>
> ***But He was wounded for our transgressions, He was bruised for our iniquities; the chastisement for our peace was upon Him, and by His stripes we are healed.***
>
> ***Isaiah 53:1-3 NKJV***

We know this passage is referring to Jesus because both Matthew (Matt.9:17) and Peter (1 Peter 2:24) refer to it. Isaiah perfectly described what Jesus would go through, and the reason why He would allow Himself to be tortured and die for us. He paid for our sin, healed our bodies and broken hearts and gave us His shalom peace.

CHAPTER ONE:

HEALING A BROKEN HEART

We all know the pain and despair of a broken heart. We have tried to sleep with tears running down our faces and soaking into the pillow, wondering if there is any hope and if anyone even cares. Well, Jesus cares, and He came to heal our broken hearts and set us free from despair.

Then Jesus returned in the power of the Spirit to Galilee and news of Him went out through all the surrounding region.

And He taught in their synagogues, being glorified by all.

So He came to Nazareth where He had been brought up. And as His custom was, He went into the synagogue on the Sabbath day and stood up to read.

And He was handed the book of the prophet Isaiah. And when He had opened the book, He found the place where it was written:

"The Spirit of the Lord is upon Me Because He has anointed Me to preach the gospel to the poor; He has sent Me to heal the broken hearted, to proclaim liberty to the captives and recovery of sight to the blind, To set at liberty those who are oppressed, to proclaim the acceptable year of the Lord."

> ***Then He closed the book and gave it back to the attendant and sat down. And the eyes of all who were in the synagogue were fixed on Him.***
>
> ***And He began to say to them, "This day this Scripture is fulfilled in your hearing."***
>
> ***Luke 4:16-21***

As we read this whole story in the other gospels we discover that because the people of Nazareth had watched Jesus grow up they had a really hard time believing He was the Son of God. They kept saying stuff like, "Isn't this the son of Joseph, the carpenter? How can He be the Messiah sent from God?" Because of their unbelief Jesus was not able to do the mighty miracles there in His home town like He had been doing in the other towns.

That had to have broken His heart. How frustrating and sad to have the power to heal and set the captives free but not be able to do anything there because they refused to believe in Him. The Bible said they were offended at Him and tried to push Him off the cliff because He proclaimed to them that He was the Messiah sent from the Father God to save them, heal them and set them free. Jesus still has the power to heal the broken heart and set the captive free, and all we need to do to receive His healing power is make the choice to love Him and believe Him in our heart as well as to believe in our minds.

That sounds strange doesn't it? But we know that if a person listens to and meditates on something long enough, it becomes part of their "hard drive". It will go from a casual thought in their mind to become resident in their heart and will begin to direct their decisions. When we believe in our hearts that our situation is hopeless and we feel we are too helpless to change anything, we make choices and say things contrary to God's Word. That is a recipe for disaster. But we have hope.

> ***But when God our Savior revealed his kindness and love, He saved us, not because of the righteous things we had done, but because of His mercy. He washed away our sins, giving us a new birth and new life through the Holy Spirit.***
>
> ***He generously poured out the Holy Spirit upon us through Jesus Christ our Savior.***
>
> ***Because of His grace, He declared us righteous and gave us confidence that we will inherit eternal life.***
>
> *Titus 3:4-7*

I have encountered the Lord's awesome grace and mercy to change and heal many times in my life. The most important time I was changed was when my Mom and Dad had taken my brothers and sisters and I to a Billy Graham meeting when I was about twelve years old. I was on my way back to my seat when suddenly the Spirit of God arrested me and moved upon my heart so very strongly to go forward during the altar call to accept Jesus as my savior.

Immediately I glanced up to the seats where my parents were sitting and thought, "What if they forget me and go home without me?" But Billy Graham had said, "Don't be afraid, your friends and family will wait for you." It was as though he heard my thoughts, but we know it was the Lord speaking through him. Fear of being abandoned and forgotten is one of the devil's favorite tricks to stop a person from moving ahead in their life.

I was pretty shy in those years and was a little afraid but the Spirit

of the Lord was so powerful upon me that I went forward and accepted Jesus as my savior. I was filled with such an awesome love, joy and peace that I have never been the same.
One day as I walked home from school I stopped to look at my friend's home and was admiring how beautiful it was. Then I realized that the home and her riches hadn't made her happy. "What would a person look for in life if riches don't make you happy?" I wondered. I played out a scene in my mind in which I was living back in the days when Jesus was on earth. I was one of His followers as He went from village to village healing the sick and setting them free from the devil. I imagined myself running ahead of Him to the next village and calling the people to come to Jesus, saying, "Jesus is coming! Bring your babies and sick ones so he can lay hands on them and heal and bless them."

Then I thought, "I would love that, but I can't go back in time to be with Jesus". Suddenly it was as though a great light burst over me and I thought, "I can do that now!" I ran home and told my mother and she began spending more time teaching me the Bible.

I remember her drawing stick figures and telling me the Bible stories and what the Lord was teaching us in these stories about our lives and how to enter the Kingdom of Heaven. I told my friends about what the Lord had done for me and that Jesus could give them the same joy and peace that I had.

Years later I received a letter from a girl who had been in my school and she reminded me that I had told her about Jesus and we had knelt by the side of the road one day on the way home from school where she accepted Jesus as her savior. She said she has walked with the Lord ever since.

I believe the Lord deposited in my heart that day a deep desire to bring people to Him, and it has never left. Jesus told His disciples in the fifteenth chapter of John that without Him we can do nothing. He also said that we can do all things through Christ (the Anointed One) who strengthens (empowers) us. (Phil. 4:13 NKJV) We must never allow the devil to deceive us into believing that we are not "good enough" to be one of Jesus' disciples and able to bring people to Jesus for salvation and deliverance. Satan uses the hurtful words and abusive things that happen to all of us when we are young to bring fear of man into our souls. It's a heartbreaking thing. I fought that fear most of my life, along with the fear of failure and fear of rejection. But Proverbs 29:25 tells us,

> ***The fear of man brings a snare, but whoever trusts in the Lord shall be safe.***
>
> ***NKJV***

We spend our lives bringing people to church to hear the Word of God and receive from the Lord, but sometimes the Lord wants us to trust Him to speak His Word through us to a soul in need. He has called each of His sons and daughters to be vessels of honor, filled with His glory and anointed to preach (declare) His gospel to all the world.

Satan will try to tell you that you are a failure and a loser and will never be able to fulfill what God has planned for your life. This is such a lie! God has told us that His power is made perfect in weakness. (See 2 Corinthians 12:9)

All we need to do is yield our lives to our Lord Jesus Christ and trust Him completely. But what does it mean to trust the Lord completely? Trust is an aspect of faith in God's integrity to keep

His word, no matter what the situation looks like.

In Mark 11:22-25 the Lord Jesus explained what faith is.

> ***So Jesus answered and said to them, "Have faith in God.***
>
> ***For assuredly I say to you, whoever says to this mountain, 'Be removed and be cast into the sea,' and does not doubt in his heart, but believes that those things he says will be done, he will have whatever he says.***
>
> ***Therefore I say to you whatever things you ask when you pray, believe that you receive them, and you will have them.***
>
> ***And whenever you stand praying, if you have anything against anyone, forgive him, that your Father in heaven may also forgive you your Trespasses."***
>
> ***NKJ***

In these verses, Jesus mentioned faith once, believing twice, and "says" three times. We need to really watch what we say! We definitely can tell how strong our faith is by the words that come out of our mouths when we are in trouble or just upset.

So, if the strength and size of our faith and the words that we speak determines the outcome of our situation, and Jesus said it does, how do we strengthen and grow our faith?

> ***And that message is the very message about faith that we preach. If you confess with your mouth that Jesus is Lord and believe in your heart that God raised Him from the dead, you will be saved. For it is by believing in your heart that you are made right with God, and it is by confessing with your mouth that you are saved. As the Scriptures tell us, "Anyone who trusts in Him will never be disgraced." Jew and Gentile are the same in this respect. They have the same Lord, Who gives generously to all who call on Him. For everyone who calls on the name of the Lord will be saved.***

But not everyone welcomes the Good News, for Isaiah the prophet said, "Lord, who has believed our message?" So faith comes from hearing, that is, hearing the Good news about Christ.

Romans 10:8-13, 16-17

Faith to Step Out

I discovered the truth of Mark 11: 22-24 when I was attending Beulah Heights Bible College in Atlanta, Georgia. This is a wonderful Bible college and most of us were about seventeen or eighteen years old, innocent and enjoying learning about life in Jesus and His kingdom. Then the devil struck. I have discovered that when you think you have learned something, maybe even got an A on a test, the real test is about to try you.

There are many stories I could tell here, but I'll just tell this one. Some kind of virus struck the area and nearly everyone was down in bed with high fever and very weak and sick. In my dorm there was not anyone who was even up and walking, much less feeling well. One of the older ladies who lived with her husband in their own apartment came over and laid hands on each one of us and prayed. I remember it so well, her hand felt so cool on my forehead because I was so hot. I didn't feel anything supernatural when she prayed, so I thought, "I guess I didn't get healed." I was so disappointed.

Then as I lay there thinking about her prayer, a sort of anger rose up in me. Not anger against God, but disgust with myself that I apparently didn't have enough faith to receive what Jesus went through such a beating to pay for.

I decided that if I was going to let my parents pay for my

schooling, and I worked after school hours to help pay for it, then I was going to believe that what I was learning was true, or I was going to leave school and go home. I remembered something we had learned in James 5:16b. The effective, fervent prayer of a righteous man avails much.

I heard the lunch bell ringing and, believe me, I was not at all hungry but I knew the Lord was speaking to my heart, asking me if I truly trusted His Word. I decided that if the Word of God was true, and it certainly was, then I was already healed whether I felt like it or not. I just said something simple like, "Well Lord, 1 Peter 2:24 does say I'm already healed by the stripes on Jesus back, so here I go!"

I managed to get out of bed and hung onto the wall to go get cleaned up and ready for lunch. I tried not to think about fainting on the way so I thought about the stories of Jesus healing people in the Bible. "He lives inside of us," I kept thinking.

In Georgia the dirt is red and if it rained, it is red mud, so I stepped on the flat walkway stones toward the dining hall. I felt so puny and lightheaded as I tried to walk, then I realized something strange. It took all my strength to take the first step because I didn't have anything to hang onto, then as I tried to take the next step, I felt an amazing strength coming up into my legs as I stepped on each stone. By the time I reached the dining hall I was completely healed!

Later on that year the student that had prayed for me gave her testimony during an assembly. She said she was just stepping out in faith on the word of God when she went to the dorms to pray for the sick. She said that I was the only one that received healing.

I thought about that and realized that something else the Word of God taught us was true. The Bible said in James 2:20-24:

> ***Don't you remember that out ancestor Abraham was shown to be right with God by his actions when he offered his son, Isaac, on the altar? You see, his faith and his actions worked together. His actions made his faith complete.***
>
> ***And so it happened just as the Scriptures say, "Abraham believed God, and God counted him as righteous because of his faith." He was even called the friend of God. So you see, we are shown to be right with God by what we do, not by faith alone.***

I don't think I received my healing because I had more faith than anyone else. We all have been given the measure of God's special faith when we accepted Jesus. I just knew the Lord was speaking to my heart and decided to obey Him and step out on His Word. After all, we all know the story of how Peter walked on the water after the Lord said to him, "Come!" He needed the Lord's word first, and then he stepped out to obey. We can do whatever the Lord tells us to do. If He hasn't told us to step out, we must continue to meditate His Word and wait for His command.

> ***For I say, through the grace given unto me, to every man that is among you, not to think of himself more highly than he ought to think; but to think soberly, according as God hath dealt to every man the measure of faith.***
>
> ***Romans 12:3(KJV)***

We had all been studying the Word of God at the Bible College, night and day, and the faith God had given us all was growing stronger and stronger in us as we meditated on His Word. After all, a baby has the same number of muscles as his father, the baby's muscles just aren't developed and strong yet. They grow stronger as babies use them.

It was the Lord that spoke to my heart and tested my faith by asking me if I believed what I had been learning. After all, you don't really know it until you <u>do</u> it. I simply chose to believe the Lord and acted on faith that I had truly heard from the Lord to step out.

I remember that miracle every time the Lord wants me to do something I am totally unable to do in my own strength. "Just take the first step, Annette, then the next one, and Jesus will help you do the rest," I tell myself. He has never let me down and He will never let you down either. Just believe His Word and take the first step in obedience to Him while holding onto His hand. That is faith. Faith is simply believing that what God said in His Word (the Bible) is the truth. God Himself said that He cannot lie. Look what He spoke through His Holy Spirit in Hebrews:

> ***For example, there was God's promise to Abraham. Since there was no one greater to swear by, God took an oath in His own name, saying:***
>
> ***I will certainly bless you, and I will multiply your descendant beyond number.***
>
> ***Geneses 22:17***
>
> ***Then Abraham waited patiently, and he received what God had promised.***
>
> ***Therefore we who have fled to Him for refuge can have great confidence as we hold to the hope that lies before us. This hope is a strong and trustworthy anchor for our souls. It leads us through the curtain into God's inner sanctuary.***
>
> ***Hebrews 6:13-15,19***

I think that the reason we sometimes have a hard time believing God's Word is true is because we have been let down so many times by people we trusted. God has promised to never let us down, however, we sometimes let ourselves down.

Aligned with God

Let me explain what I mean by that. I have attended a wonderful Assembly of God Church that taught classes on healing our wounded soul. One of the classes that really spoke to me was a class concerning being "aligned" with God and His Word rather than our wounded emotions.

That teaching reminded me of a vision a wonderful teacher and pastor had received from the Lord concerning his own wounded soul after his wife died.

In the vision he saw a bountiful outpouring of fruit from Heaven toward a cornucopia on a table. However, the cornucopia was not in alignment to receive the fruit, it was lying on its side and the fruit was tumbling over it and falling from the table. The Lord explained to him that he was the cornucopia and his meditation on his grief and depression kept him from receiving the blessings the Lord so much wanted to pour out on him to heal his heart. He said he couldn't understand why it was that when he had prayed for others, they received their healing but his wife didn't.

I was so thankful that the pastor humbled himself and was so transparent to share that vision with the church because it has helped me tremendously over the years. I watched that pastor seek the face of Jesus and receive the joy of the Lord and His strength to continue to be the excellent pastor and teacher the Lord called him to be. That pastor teaches in an excellent Bible School and it is so wonderful to attend a powerful Bible School and learn the Word of God. But it is even more inspiring to watch it being modeled and acted out before our eyes by the teacher. It has been said that true faith is acting like God's Word is true.

Over the years, when my heart was wounded, I asked the Lord to keep me in alignment with Him and His Word. His Holy Spirit can then help me love and forgive and go forward, trusting God's faithfulness. How do we stay in alignment with Jesus and His Word? One of the ways that helps me is by imagining myself walking with Jesus and listening to Him as He taught His disciples.

Our imagination is more powerful than we realize. We know we should meditate the Word of God, which is to read it aloud and softly murmur or "mutter" it for a while until it becomes part of us. But we have to be careful that it is not just memorized in our mind without becoming part of our core being, or our heart. That is no more helpful than if a parrot recited a scripture. That is where our imagination comes in. Jesus said if a person lusted after a person and imagined himself committing a sexual sin with them, it was the same as if he had actually done it.

So if that works in the negative sense, it also works in the positive. Think about Abraham walking up Mt. Moriah with Isaac to sacrifice him.

> ***By faith Abraham, when he was tested, offered up Isaac, and he who had received the promises offered up his only begotten son, of whom it was said, "In Isaac your seed shall be called," concluding that God***

was able to raise him up, even from the dead, from which he also received him in a figurative sense. (Image, or in his mind's imagination)

Hebrews 11:19 (parentheses mine)

It is so vitally important that we see ourselves in our imagination winning the battle and passing the test even before the test begins. Then that picture will be formed in our hearts. Jesus said many times that we should have eyes to see and ears to hear so we can believe. These are spiritual eyes.

The only way we can have this kind of faith in God and His promises is to catch a vision of how faithful and true God is and how much He loves us. We must see ourselves as He sees us, more precious than silver or gold or any kind of jewel. He sees the beautiful jewel underneath the junk that has to be carefully cleaned away.

I have always had trouble seeing myself as precious and beautiful. Even as a small child. So, as I began to read and study God's Word, I would imagine myself as one of the children that Jesus would hold on His lap as He taught the disciples. If Jesus thinks children are precious when they haven't done anything to earn His approval, then I told myself that I was precious also. Now sometimes that takes faith.

It is Jesus Who makes us valuable and worthy when we accept Him as Lord and Savior. Not after we do awesome things for Him, but at the moment He comes into our heart, we belong to Him and He has already made us worthy.

That is also the moment that His love fills our hearts and we long to follow Him everywhere He goes and become just like Him. He begins to teach us who we actually are now that we are in Him and He is in us.

The Light of the World

Jesus said that He is the light of the world. Just think, that awesome Light now lives in us. We are jars of clay containing glorious light in a very dark world. This Light lives in our spirit, but our minds still need to be renewed to understand this and be transformed. Satan, who is the god of this world, has blinded the minds of those who don't believe. They are unable to see the glorious light of the Good News. They don't understand this message about the glory of Christ, Who is the exact likeness of God.

> ***For God, Who said, "Let there be light in the darkness," has made this light shine in our hearts so we could know the glory of God that is seen in the face of Jesus Christ.***
>
> ***We now have this light shining in our hearts, but we ourselves are like fragile clay jars containing this great treasure. This makes it clear that our great power is from God, not from ourselves.***
>
> ***2 Corinthians 4:4-10.***

We are now in the process of being recreated into a golden "vessel of honor, fit for the Master's use."

But God's truth stands firm like a foundation stone with this inscription: "The LORD knows those who are His," and "All who belong to the LORD must turn away from evil."

In a wealthy home some utensils are made of gold and silver, and some are made of wood and clay. The expensive utensils are used for special occasions, and the cheap ones are for everyday use. If you keep yourself pure, you will be a special utensil for honorable use. Your life will be clean, and you will be ready for the Master to use you for every good work.

2 Timothy 2:20-21

If someone defiled that vessel and the vessel was able to speak to the Master to be cleansed, the Master would tenderly take the vessel and cleanse it. It would not stop being the Master's precious vessel. However, if the vessel had free will and chose not to repent of its part in the defilement, it would not be fit for the Master's use any longer until it did repent.

Our spirit, as a child of God, has been purified and the Holy Spirit is dwelling in us. However, our minds can be defiled by allowing wrong thoughts and wrong imaginations. We must immediately tell the Lord that we repent and change our ways and thoughts and cast them out. We have the ability to do that by speaking the Word of God in place of the wrong thought or wrong attitude. We may have to do it more than once if that wrong imagination has started to grow roots.

When I first started Bible College the Lord gave me a mini vision to help me understand why He had brought me there. I was sitting in bed studying and discussing it all with the Lord. (I don't know if you would call it praying, but I was asking Him questions.)

Suddenly I saw a vision of myself standing and looking straight ahead. Jesus was on my right side and the devil was on my left. I saw that when I looked at Jesus, I found myself leaning toward

Him, but if I looked at the devil, I found myself leaning toward him. That was the end of the vision, but I understood immediately. Jesus is called the Word of God in John 1:1, and as we study and meditate His Word, we lean toward Him, love and obey Him, and begin to become like Him. As we worship Him, He fills our hearts with His love, love for Him and love for others.

The same is true of the devil for evil. When we watch TV shows about murder, illicit sex, strife in marriages and families, etc., our imagination becomes warped and we find bitter thoughts beginning to grow roots in our minds.

> ***Work at living in peace with everyone, and work at living a holy life, for those who are not holy will not see the Lord. Look after each other so that none of you fails to receive the grace of God. Watch out that no poisonous root of bitterness grows up to trouble you, corrupting many.***
>
> ***Hebrews 12:15***

When I was in the tenth grade my parents were moving back to our house in Florida, and I didn't want to go. So they sent me to a Bible College and High School combined in Canada. While I was there we learned a poem that really spoke to me. I don't remember the author but I do remember the first line:

> ***Man, earthy of the earth, an hungered feeds on earth's dark bitter roots and poison weeds.***

God has given us free will and we can choose to feed on earth's bitter roots and poison weeds, or we can choose to feed on God's Word. And what we choose to think on and feed upon, determines the outcome of our lives.

If we just look at the bad situation with our natural knowledge and understanding we might just give up in fear and despair. But God has not given us a spirit of fear, but of power, love and a sound mind. (See 2 Timothy 1:7). We have been given the ability to choose; fear of the facts before our eyes or faith in God's Word? Our lives depend on which one we choose.

When I was working at TCT, WAQP TV, I hurt my leg and the pain was excruciating, to the point that I had to have a volunteer come in to help me at my job.

During that time there was a prayer partner that worked on the prayer lines who was facing cancer surgery. Benny Hinn was ministering communion and the Word of God in another state and my sister and I believed the Lord wanted us to take the prayer partner to that state for the communion service because she strongly believed in the power of the Word of God and communion.

Just before we left, her doctor told her the surgery was scheduled for the same time and she was unable to go. She asked us to go anyway and as we took communion, hold her up in prayer. We made the choice to go and we drove to the meeting, even though all the while I was in awful pain. We chose to believe God's Word and that it was His will for us to go, knowing He would help me climb all those steps without falling. In my mind and heart I bound up fear and threw it out the window and chose to focus on my faith in God's character of truth and faithfulness.

When we took the shuttle from the hotel to the convention center and I tried to go up the steps of the shuttle my leg collapsed and I fell, right in front of everyone. I didn't let that stop me and at the convention center my sister and I prayed for a seat nearby, not

100 steps up! We walked into the auditorium, and lo and behold, there were two seats right there on that level at the end of the row. I didn't have to climb or go down steps at all! Miracle number one!

As we took communion and prayed for the prayer partner, the presence of the Lord was so powerful and sweet and I knew she would receive her healing (and she did!). Miracle number two! At the end of our prayer for her I just tossed in a quick request that the Lord would heal my leg also.

When it was time for our shuttle to come get us, I hated to leave but we had to go so we hurried out the door and I waited on a bench with our Bibles and purses as my sister watched for the shuttle. When she waved to me that it was there I grabbed our stuff and ran across the parking lot and ran up the steps of the bus. As I sat beside my sister I suddenly realized, I had been healed and didn't even know it! What a good God we serve! What if I had chosen to stay home because of my pain? Think about it. Faith chooses obedience!

David had to face down the lion and bear before the Lord sent him to face down Goliath. When we don't understand why we have to face a hurtful situation, we must know beyond a shadow of doubt that God will help us overcome and our faith will grow in the process. Then when we face the giants in our lives, we have a faith in Father God that has grown from a tiny mustard seed to a giant tree. We can then speak to that giant in great faith and bring it down in the Name of Jesus.

CHAPTER TWO

GOD'S LOVE CASTS OUT OF FEAR

"There is no fear in love; but perfect love casts out fear: because fear hath torment. He that fears is not made perfect in love."

1 John 4:18 KJV

There were so many miraculous rescues in my life as I was growing up. During my fifth and eighth grade I lived in a small community and attended a school that was out in the country. The school yard was fenced in and we were told not to cross the fence. However, one day my girlfriends persuaded me to cross over while we were waiting for the bus to come at the end of the day.

No sooner were we over the fence and into the woods looking for flowers when a gang of rough guys jumped out of the bushes, hooting with laughter, and started to grab the girls. I stared, horrified, at the other girls and saw they were laughing and cutting their eyes over at me, and I realized it was a set-up. I found out later that my best friend's brother, the leader of the gang, liked me and she had set it up for him. Some of the girls were going off into the woods and bushes with the guys and I knew I had to get out of there.

"Jesus!" I breathed, and suddenly I knew He would help me if I believed Him instead of letting fear of the guys overtake me. I yelled, “Look! Is that the bus?” They all stopped and looked over at the road and I ran for the fence as fast as I could go. They were right behind me, running faster than I could ever run. All I could do was call out, “Jesus!” and keep running. When I got to the fence I knew I didn’t have time to stop and climb up so I just put my hands on the top of the fence, which was chest high, and suddenly I supernaturally flew over it and kept running without a stumble. They had to stop and climb over so I was able to make it to the school and run into the girl’s restroom locking the door, safe.

Another time I was sent to get something out of a storage room and someone locked the door. Suddenly I heard a snicker and I discovered the gang leader was hiding in there. He said, “Hey there, how about a little kiss?”

My mom and dad had taught us the power of the Name of Jesus and I breathed, “Jesus, help me”. Then courage filled me and I told him that he had better let me out or he would be in trouble with God and His angels. He laughed but never tried to touch me, just tried to persuade me to kiss him. Finally, he let me out (someone must have unlocked the door). I doubt if he would have harmed me, but I was a very shy little girl and this gang frightened me with all the tricks they constantly pulled.

That gang leader would beat my brother up nearly every day and tell me that he would stop if I would give him a kiss. My brother took the beatings and never once asked me to kiss the guy so he would leave him alone. I have loved and admired my brother all my life.

At first it amazed me that many years later my brother still loved that state and bought land right in that area, when I had such bad memories of that place. That was one of the memories that Jesus had to heal in my soul. Now I love that place. It may have been so traumatic because of the obvious betrayal of one of my friends, to always set me up for these scary situations. I think it was so scary because the gang leader would tell me in very plain terms what he wanted to do to me. Looking back I realized he probably never would have harmed me, but at the time I was frightened of him.

Many years later, when I was in a Christian Bible College and High School in Canada, I received a letter from that same guy. I have no idea how he even got the address where I was. My roommate encouraged me to write back to him but I was afraid to begin any contact and correspondence with him. I am so sorry now that I let fear stop me from witnessing to him of God's love for him. We must always guard our hearts from fear of betrayal and fear of man. Just when we think we have conquered the fear of man, it will try to sneak up on us from another direction.

I think all of us can look back on our lives and realize how the Lord constantly rescued us from the power of darkness. He rescues us because He loves us so much, but we must use these incidents to declare His love and power to those who don't know Him like we do. We must ask Him to take us beyond thankfulness of our survival and allow Him to use our stories of rescue to lead others to Him.

I wish I could say that fear of betrayal and harm was instantly and miraculously removed from my soul as I studied the Word of God, but I can see that it was a daily walk with God, learning to totally trust Him, step by step. I believe my fear of sudden attack was caused by an attempted rape at the age of three. A young teenage guy caught me in my parent's barn hay loft after my older sisters had already gone to the house. He held me down, holding his hand over my mouth as he tried to molest me.

I was terrified and I believe an angel came to help me because the guy suddenly ran away without actually raping me. I remembered the incident all my life and I had thought I was probably around the age of three when it happened because I hadn't started school yet. Many years later a prophetess who didn't know me spoke into my life and said Satan had tried to attack me many times in my life, beginning at age three, but Jesus had always delivered me. So I know I was three when that happened, but I wasn't too young to know that Jesus loved me and would protect me.

I remember that Mom and Dad would pray with us every night and have "family devotions", teaching us the stories in the Word of God of His love and protection. They always taught us to ask the Lord for help when we were in trouble and He would help us.

What Satan meant for evil, God turned for good because I grew up knowing that when I cried out to Jesus for help, He would always send His angels to deliver me. However, I still had to fight the fear of a sudden attack coming from an unknown place or person. I had a difficult time trusting people. I love the Ninety First Psalm. I have held onto that Psalm over the years, reading and quoting it to renew my faith in God's faithfulness to deliver me in danger. There are so many wonderful stories of people that quoted that psalm in danger and were miraculously saved from harm and death.

I think a lot of us have heard of the officer in the war that asked his men under him to join him in quoting that psalm before a battle. Not one soldier in that group was killed or injured even though they were all in fierce battles many times. However, I had also heard someone talking about a soldier who constantly quoted that psalm in battle even though he was terrified. They talked about how great it was that he still quoted the psalm, over and over, no matter what danger they were in. Unfortunately, he was killed.

I asked the Lord what the difference was in the two soldiers and the strong thought came to me that the terrified soldier was trusting in the psalm like an amulet or charm, whereas the officer was trusting in the Lord of the psalm. They both had faith in God, but sometimes if we focus too much on what we are afraid of, it blocks our faith from being effective. The Word of God can be spoken, but if we allow the fear and unbelief to dominate our thinking, our confession of the Word becomes no more powerful than a tape player or parrot speaking.

> ***For indeed the gospel was preached to us as well as to them, but the word which they heard did not profit them, not being mixed with faith in those who heard it.***
>
> ***Heb. 4:1-2 NKJV***

> ***But without faith it is impossible to please Him, for he who comes to God must believe that HE IS, and that He is a rewarded of those who diligently seek Him.***
>
> ***Hebrews 11:6 NKJV***

> ***And we know that faith works by love.***
>
> ***Galatians 5:6***

It wasn't until years later that I learned to completely forgive the betrayers and to ask the Lord for His compassion for hurtful people, for they are usually hurting people, covering a foundation of fear. It is through forgiveness that faith, working by love, begins to cast out fear.

When we abide in His love we can then learn to love others, and we are able to dwell in the secret place of the Most High. The Psalm 91 promises are for those who dwell in that secret place. Read it all.

> ***He who dwells in the secret place of the Most High shall abide under the shadow of the Almighty.***
>
> ***Because he has set his love upon Me, therefore will I deliver him;***
>
> ***I will set him on high, because he knows and understands My name (has a personal knowledge of My mercy, love and kindness—trusts and relies on Me, knowing I will never forsake him, no, never).***
>
> ***He shall call upon Me and I will answer him. I will be with him in trouble; I will deliver him and honor him.***
>
> ***With long life I will satisfy him, and show him My salvation.***
>
> ***Psalm 91:1,14-16 AMP***

These ae such wonderful promises, spoken from a God Who doesn't lie. He always keeps His Word because His Word is based on His blood covenant that He cut with His only begotten Son, Jesus, on the cross of Calvary.

When we accept Jesus as Savior, ask Him to come into our heart and become Lord of our lives, we then have entered into blood covenant with our Father God through Jesus' shed blood on the cross. The study of our blood covenant is awesome.

Why then do Christians sometimes fall into evil situations? I don't begin to know all the reasons, but this Psalm begins with a condition, it is dwelling in the secret place of the Most High. It also says it is because you have made the LORD, Who is my refuge, even the Most High, your dwelling place. Not just a visiting place when we don't have anything else to do. Or we are in trouble. So, what is the secret of the "secret place of the Most High?" I believe it is found in Matthew 22:36-40. KJV

> ***Master, which is the great commandment in the law? Jesus said unto him, "Thou shalt love the LORD thy God with all thy heart, with all thy soul and with all thy mind. This is the first and great commandment.***
>
> ***And the second is like unto it: Thou shalt love thy neighbor as thyself.***
> ***On these two commandments hang all the Law and the Prophets".***

These verses mean so much to me and I try to always measure the maturity of my life by them. One great teacher on TV told a vision the Lord had given him about these scriptures. He said that he saw a vision from the Lord of a man who was trying to hang curtains to a window without a curtain rod. He said that at first the antics of the man were so humorous that he laughed out loud. The man would put a curtain up to the window and when it would fall he would get all twisted up in the curtain and end up falling himself. Then he would try again with another curtain and would find himself rolling within the curtain along the floor.

It was humorous and the teacher laughed at the man's antics, until he saw little snakes nipping at the man's heels. Then it wasn't funny anymore. Suddenly the teacher watching this vision realized that there were names written on each curtain. One said healing, another said deliverance, and a third curtain said prosperity, and so on.

The man trying to hang the curtains began to cry out to God in an agonized voice, saying, "God! I believe in healing and deliverance and prosperity! Why do I always fail to receive what I know You paid for? Then the teacher watching the vision became aware of a huge golden curtain rod in the corner of the room. It was as big as a bridge girder, and he suddenly knew that the man hanging the curtains was also aware of the rod and the words written on it. The words written on the rod were those we saw earlier,

> ***"Thou shalt love the Lord thy God with all thy heart, and with all thy soul, and with all thy mind. This is the first and great commandment. And the second is like unto it, thou shalt love thy neighbor as thyself. On these two commandments hang all the law and the prophets."***
>
> ***Matthew 22:37-40 (KJV)***

Suddenly a loud booming voice echoed around the room, saying; "Hang the rod, not the curtains! The curtains are connected to the rod!" Wow! That sure drew a picture for me of the importance of allowing God's unconditional love to fill my heart and pour out to those around me. Not only does our love affect the lives of those in our family and our co- workers, it also affects our ability to receive God's blessings that He has already paid for.

So, what do the scriptures mean when they say that faith works by love? (See Galatians 5:6) Well, for one thing, we can only trust God when we truly know that He loves us unconditionally. Love that is conditional is not pure love and cannot be trusted. I heard a speaker years ago when I was in Tulsa, Oklahoma speak about God's pure, unconditional love that brought us our salvation. I have heard some of the best speakers teach about the love of God, but the truth of this message pierced my heart that day. I realized that I was always trying to be good enough to cause God to love me. But all the time He loved me just the way I was.

Does that mean I live my life just any way I want to and I automatically am saved and go to heaven when I die? I tell you what, if committing sin doesn't bother you, you probably don't really know the Lord. When you truly know Him in an intimate way, you fall in love with Him and it hurts you to sin because you know sin hurts Him. You must believe in your heart that Jesus is truly the Son of God and that He loved you so much that He was willing to die a horrible death on the cross to take your sin and give you His righteousness, His "right standing" with God.

You must believe in your heart that He truly did rise from the dead by the glory of God and He told His disciples before He ascended to Heaven that He was coming again to take us to live with Him forever. We must also believe that our salvation is not based on how good we are, because we can never be good enough. The Holy Spirit speaks to our hearts and convicts us of sin and at the same time reveals God's awesome love that He has for us. It is the revelation of that love that causes us to ask Him to cleanse our hearts from sin by the blood of the Lamb of God that takes away the sin of the world. (See John 1:29) Everyone knows John 3:16, but let's look at the verses before and after that verse.

> ***Jesus answered, "Most assuredly I say to you, unless one is born of water and the Spirit, he cannot enter the Kingdom of God. That which is born of the flesh is flesh and that which is born of the Spirit is spirit.***
>
> ***Do not marvel that I said to you, 'You must be born again.' And as***

Moses lifted up the serpent in the wilderness, even so must the Son of Man be lifted up, that whoever believes in Him should not perish but have eternal life.

For God so loved the world that He gave His only begotten Son, that whoever believes in Him should not perish but have everlasting life.

For God did not send His Son into the world to condemn the world, but that the world through Him might be saved.

He who believes in Him is not condemned, but he who does not believe is condemned already because he has not believed in the name of the only begotten Son of God."

John 3:5-7, 14-18 NKJV

In John 3:16, the verb form of the word "loved" is *agapao,* which, according to Strong's #25, means unconditional love, love by choice and by an act of the will. The word denotes unconquerable benevolence and undefeatable goodwill. Agapao will never seek anything but the highest good for fellow mankind. *Agapao* (the verb), and *agape* (the noun) are the words for God's unconditional love. It does not need a feeling or a chemistry. It is a word that exclusively belongs to the Christian community.

Unconditional love seems almost "too good to be true", and actually is too good to be true for our natural self-centered lives to give. Only when we accept Jesus as Savior and Lord of our lives can we "download" His love into our hearts and allow this love to flow out to others.

Look and Live!

Jesus said that just as the serpent as lifted up in the wilderness, so must the Son of Man be lifted up. The story behind that statement was quite awesome. God had brought the children of Israel out of Egypt through many miracles and was taking them to the Promised Land, but they complained all the way there. They even had the gall to accuse God and Moses of bringing them to the wilderness to die.

They were sick and tired of the manna that God sent down from heaven every day for them to eat, and in Numbers 21:6 they said that they hated that bread. So because of their blaming and complaining the Lord allowed fiery serpents to bite the people and many of them died. In verse seven the Bible said that they came to Moses and confessed;

> ***Therefore the people came to Moses and said," We have sinned, for we have spoken against the LORD and against thee. Pray unto the LORD that He take away the serpents from us." And Moses prayed for the people.***
>
> ***And the LORD said unto Moses, "Make thee a fiery serpent and set it upon a pole; and it shall come to pass that everyone who is bitten, when he looketh upon it, shall live."***
>
> ***So Moses made a serpent of brass and put it upon a pole; and it came to pass that if a serpent had bitten anyone, when he beheld the serpent of brass, he lived.***
>
> ***Num. 21:8-9 KJV***

Moses' fiery serpent on the pole was a picture or type of Jesus on the cross and since a serpent or snake is a picture of sin, Jesus became sin for us so we could become the righteousness of God in Christ Jesus. (2 Corinthians 5:21)
All they had to do was to look at the fiery serpent and they would live and not die. Try to imagine what was happening there in the

wilderness. Suppose you were a parent and the serpents were everywhere, biting anyone they could get their fangs into. You would be screaming for help and grabbing your children and running wildly, only to run into another snake hiding behind a rock. Your child would be screaming, "Mommy, the snake bit me! I'm going to die, help me!

When you are in trouble like that, you simply don't have time to work out a formal and beautiful prayer to God. You simply cry out to God, "Save me!" And what does He say? "Look and live!" You may wonder why God would allow fiery serpents to come and bite them in the first place. I thought about that when I was in Bible College, and I realized that it was not a small thing to blaspheme God like that when all He was trying to do was get them out of slavery in Egypt and get the slavery mentality out of them before He could bring them into their Promised Land. They had been protected from danger in the wilderness by God's power but their evil words brought them out from under God's protection.

God doesn't just have love, He is love. Everything He does in our lives is based on love. It may not seem like it at the time, but it's true. When we walk away from Him, we walk out of His blessings and bring all kinds of hurtful things upon ourselves. Then instead of crying out to Him for help and repenting of our sin, we have a tendency to blame Him for it. "Were you not paying attention, Lord, when I fell into that sewage ditch?" We fail to realize that we fell into the sewage ditch because our eyes were gazing on something they shouldn't have been on in the first place.

We have always been taught that the meaning of sin is to miss the mark. It also means to take the wrong path. Unfortunately, the wrong path has a cliff at the end of it or a trap laid by the devil. God puts signs up all along the way, "Don't take this path! Stay straight on the path I have shown you." The devil also puts his signs up. "Take this path, I have such fun waiting for you along the way." The trouble is, his "fun" ends in disaster and ultimately death.

Sometimes the devil's path is so disguised with pretty flowers and delicious looking fruit that we have a hard time deciding if this is God's path or the devil's. At this point we must stop and pray for wisdom and guidance before we make our decision. This is vital! Don't think we have to hear a voice from heaven to tell us the way to go. His Word is an awesome road map and the Holy Spirit will lead and guide us in His still small voice.

Then when the Lord speaks to our hearts and we really feel a check to not go there, we must never disregard that nudge from the Lord, thinking, "Well, I'm sure that was just me. The Lord wants me to have a good life with lots of fun and money, etc. The Lord wants me to have a really good looking and fun mate, and I'm sure this is the right one." Maybe not! The devil offers his brand of "love," but it is poison love. Some poison can really taste good but the pain and death is just not worth it.

I found something I wrote a long time ago about the difference between God's agape love and the devil's poison love. "Toxic love will always focus on self. Agape love is the God kind of love and is focused on helping others." This is what I have been teaching in the counseling classes for couples before the marriage ceremony. This message of God's agape, unconditional love is burning inside me like Jeremiah's "fire in my bones."

We simply cannot truly love our mate or others with God's agape unconditional love unless we have His love deposited in our hearts first. We know the Bible says that "God is love." If we want God's kind of love, we must not only accept His salvation by faith, but we must also accept His Lordship. That means Jesus is King of His kingdom. We must trust Him to be the kind of king that loves us and knows what is best for us.

Have you ever met a "Christian" who is mean as a snake? They may have never actually accepted Jesus' salvation, but if so, they have never made Him Lord of their lives. There is a spiritual throne in our hearts and the king of our lives sits on that throne and makes the rules and decisions. We need to check and see if we ourselves are sitting on that throne and "it's all about me" (I actually heard someone say that once).

When we enter the Kingdom of God and become a child of God, the Lord begins to gently teach us that this kingdom is not a democracy, it's a kingdom and we obey because He is King and He loves us and we love Him. We don't vote. I keep dwelling on this because it made such a difference in my life when this truth pierced my heart. I had done way too much "voting" in my life. I figured out what I thought was best for me and neglected to ask the Lord what He wanted in certain situations. That never turns out well.

Jesus gave us free will, and our will is generally very strong, even from childhood. The idea of giving someone else authority over our lives, even the Lord, Who loves us more than we can even imagine, can be very scary. We may have a tendency to think, "What if He asks me to do something I don't want to do or I'm afraid to do?" Count on it. He will and He does, in order to take away our fears as we trust Him and obey Him. He loves to make us face our fears and overcome them.

We are born with the instinct to protect ourselves and we do it automatically. That means always being in control, whether we realize we're doing it or not. The following verses can be really hard to understand and obey if we are not really in love with Jesus. Look at what Jesus taught in Matthew 5:38-48

> ***You have heard the law that says the punishment must match the injury: "An eye for an eye, and a tooth for a tooth. But I say, do not resist an evil person! If someone slaps you on the right cheek, offer the other cheek also. If you are sued in court and your shirt is taken from you, give your coat too. If a soldier demands that you carry his gear for a mile, carry it two miles. Give to those who ask, and don't turn away from those who want to borrow.***
>
> ***You have heard the law that says, "Love your neighbor and hate your enemy. But I say, love your enemies! Pray for those who persecute you! In that way you will be acting as true children of your Father in heaven. For He gives His sunlight to both the evil and the good and He sends rain on the just and the unjust alike. If you love only those who love you, what reward is there for that? Even corrupt tax collectors do that much. If you are kind only to your friends, how are you different from anyone else? Even pagans do that. But you are to be perfect, even as your Father in heaven is perfect.***

WHAT! I can just hear it now. First of all, how can anyone be perfect as Father God? The word "perfect" here means to be grown up, mature and whole, not self-centered, childish, and no longer fragmented and broken. Only Jesus can do that in us and for us as we trust Him enough to submit to Him.

The devil does everything he can to persuade us that God doesn't want the best for us. The devil comes to us as "an angel of light," trying to draw us down his path of destruction. He really was Lucifer in heaven, which means an angel of light, however, he is no longer an angel of light although he tries to appear to us as one. He is a fallen angel of darkness and death. We must recognize his tricks and resist him.

I have often thought of the angels that believed Lucifer and turned on God, thinking that the devil's lies were right and they could take God's throne. How stupid! God is so loving and kind that even they forgot that He is also all powerful! We would never be so stupid, would we? So, who is sitting on the throne of your heart? That throne belongs to God alone.

I thank God for His grace to forgive us and give us the strength to overcome our weaknesses when we repent.

> ***But He gives us even more grace to stand against such evil desires. As the Scriptures say,***
>
> ***"God opposes the proud but favors (gives grace to) the humble." So humble yourselves before God, resist the devil, and he will flee from you. Come close to God, and God will come close to you.***
>
> ***James 4:3-7 NLT***

I looked up the meaning of the word submit and it literally means to stand under. This suggests obedience, submission and subjection as well as humility. I believe it is vitally important that we humble ourselves under the mighty hand of God and He will then lift us up. (See James 4:10) This is a person who is willingly submitted to God and His will.

It isn't true humility if the submission is not willing. Forced submission is not true submission and true humility. And we can only submit willingly and even joyfully when we truly love God. When we willingly and lovingly humble ourselves before God and resist the devil, he will flee from us. We have the power inside us to overcome the devil. That power is not our natural strength, it is the power of the Holy Spirit Who came to live in us when we accepted Jesus as our Savior, Lord and King.

We do not have to be afraid of the devil. The Lion of the tribe of Judah lives in us! We must never submit to the devil and his evil desires. Naturally speaking, submission and humility are not excitingly wonderful words. They bring a picture of bowing your neck to a bully who steals your lunch money at school and then runs away with his buddies laughing while you walk away angry and hungry. But that is not the way Jesus sees you. He sees you holding your head up and trusting the Lord to deliver you in the midst of every evil enemy.

I heard a minister tell his story about bullies in his school when he was young who constantly shoved him and his friends around and took their lunch money. He told his father about it, who then talked to him about who he was in Christ Jesus. His father reminded him that he must love his enemies, not fear them. He realized that as a child of the King of Kings, he didn't have to submit to the devil and the devil's buddies, he just needed to submit himself to the Lord, resist the devil and he would flee.

The next day he was in school he was ready and waiting. As the bullies came toward him he squared his shoulders planning to stand up to them. He had his scriptures all ready to quote to them and tell them that he was a child of the King of Kings and he loved them with God's love, but they couldn't have his lunch money!

As they got closer to him, he started to grin and then laugh, thinking about how surprised they would be when he stood up to them. The more he thought about Jesus and His angels helping him, the more he laughed. The bullies stopped and stared at him and suddenly they turned and walked away, all nervous because he was standing there looking at them and laughing. He didn't even have to say anything. He submitted himself to God and they really did flee! That is truly awesome.

Jesus is our perfect example of willing and loving submission to the Heavenly Father's will. Look at Philippians 2:5-11 NLT

> ***Is there any encouragement from belonging to Christ? Any comfort from His love? Then make me truly happy by agreeing wholeheartedly with each other; loving one another and working together with one mind and purpose.***
>
> ***Don't be selfish; don't try to impress others. Be humble, thinking of others as better than yourselves. Don't look out only for you own interests, but take an interest in others too. You must have the same attitude that Christ Jesus had.***
>
> ***Though He was God, He did not think of equality with God as something to cling to. Instead He gave up his divine privileges; He took the humble position of a slave and was born as a human being.***
>
> ***When He appeared in human form He humbled Himself in obedience to God and died a criminal's death on a cross. Therefore, God elevated Him to the place of highest honor and gave Him the name above all other names, that at the name of Jesus every knee***

should bow in heaven and on earth and every tongue confess that Jesus Christ is Lord, to the glory of God the Father.

Jesus did this because He loved us and because He loved His Father and wanted to submit to His Father's will, even at the cost of dying and going to hell in order to save us. It is God's love inside us that causes us to die to our own will and submit to God's will in our lives, even when our natural selves don't want to.

It is also God's will for us to love others just as He loves us. Naturally speaking, that is easier said than done. In our own strength, it is almost impossible to love a bully, even a husband that we promised before God to love and cherish until death parts us. Or trying to love and cherish a wife that tries to always get her own way by being controlling and manipulating everyone.

Psychologists pretty much all agree that bossy domineering people have a core base of fear in their hearts, caused by some threatening trauma in their past. They hide their fear in different ways, such as sarcasm, hurtful words, or an "I don't care" attitude, the fear is still there, making them miserable as well as everyone else.

Fear of rejection is most people's greatest fear because love is our greatest need. This causes such great pain that we even imagine rejection when it isn't even true. How can we truly love people as God tells us to if we look at them through a filter of fear and keep a wall around us for protection against the rejection. I know because that was the way I was for years; until I fell deeply in love with Jesus.

When I was young there was a recurring thought that would come to me when I was alone or washing dishes, or just before I went to sleep. I would suddenly have a deep yearning desire to know the Lord in a more intimate way, and I would think, "I wish I could walk with God like Enoch walked with God."

I remember I would immediately scoff at myself, and say to myself, "Boy, God sure must have laughed at that prayer! I could never be good enough to walk with God!" I didn't realize He had placed that desire in my heart. But the Lord never gave up on me.He just kept loving me and calling me to a higher walk with Him. The more I studied the Word of God, especially the book of John, I began to see Jesus. Not just know about Him to pass my tests in Bible School, but to fall in love with Him. As He poured His love into me, I began to love other people with His love, not conditional love.

Jesus is calling us to love Him unconditionally and as He fills us with His love, we begin to love others with His love. This is a miracle because we grow up from childhood learning to protect our hearts from people who hurt us with damaging, negative words.

So, how can we possible give love unconditionally to an abusive person? We can't in our own strength. We're just too afraid. We unconsciously think, "If I love this dude when he is acting like such a jerk, he will walk all over me! I have to stand up for myself! If I don't, no one else will!" That is victim mentality acting out as a bully. We have forgotten that when we give the situation and people into Jesus' hands, He will stand up for us. We can stand tall in His strength and authority and still love that dude without being abusive in defense.

Unfortunately, that was the victim slave mentality that the Children of Israel had in the wilderness when they were blaming Moses and God for everything. God told them He would take care of them and bring them into a good land, flowing with milk and honey. But did they trust Him? Look at Exodus 3:5-8

> ***Then He (God) said, "Do not draw near this place. Take your sandals off your feet for the place where you stand is holy ground.***
>
> ***Moreover He said, "I am the God of your father—the God of Abraham, the God of Isaac, and the God of Jacob." And Moses hid his face for he was afraid to look upon God.***
>
> ***And the LORD said, "I have surely seen the oppression of My people who are in Egypt, and have heard their cry because of their taskmasters, for I knows their sorrows.***
> ***So I have come down to deliver them out of the hand of the Egyptians, and to bring them up from that land to a good and large land flowing with milk and honey."***

So I ask you, if God Himself came down and visited us in a burning bush and told us He would deliver us out of our mess and bring us into a wonderful place, if it was a little rough along the way, would we complain and blaspheme His name like they did? I truly hope not. To blaspheme His name is to speak evil of His character. They didn't know that He loved them. They had never known loving kindness and compassion, so when they got thirsty or hungry they were afraid that God would let them down. They thought they had to whine and complain or be aggressive to bully God and Moses to listen to them in order to get their needs met.

Have you ever known anyone like that? Have compassion on them because they are very insecure, which is a facet of fear of failure and rejection. The Lord told me that once about a supervisor that I had in a Christian organization. I cried out to the Lord one day and said, "Don't managers and supervisors have to live by 1 Corinthians 13 like everybody else?"

He answered me in a loving and gentle voice I could hear clearly and said, "Yes, but don't forget the rest of that chapter." He then was silent but I knew He was listening to my thoughts. I remembered that ***love suffers long and is kind, does not behave rudely, does not seek its own, is not provoked, thinks no evil.*** He then said clearly, "***Be patient with her, she is very insecure.***" I can still hear His voice and it was so patient and loving. That is when I truly learned that when He speaks a word to you, that word carries in it the power to bring it to pass. When He told me to be patient with her, He imparted that patience to me, along with His love for her.

The next Monday at work she came into my room and slapped some papers on my desk without a word or a "Good morning" or even a smile and then turned around and swished out. The other girl in the room said to me, "How can you *stand* her?" I answered from God's love in my heart, "Be patient with her, she's very insecure." I felt nothing but love and compassion for her, and later on we became good friends. That is what God can do when He imparts His agape love in our hearts by the Holy Spirit.

CHAPTER THREE

FRUIT OF THE SPIRIT

When you follow the desires of your sinful nature, the results are very clear; sexual immorality, impurity, lustful pleasures, idolatry, sorcery, hostility, quarreling, jealousy, outbursts of anger, selfish ambition, dissension, division, envy, drunkenness, wild parties, and other sins like these.

Let me tell you again, as I have before, that anyone living that sort of life will not inherit eternal life.

But the Holy Spirit produces this kind of fruit in our lives: love, joy, peace, patience, kindness, goodness, faithfulness, gentleness and self-control. There is no law against these things!

Gal. 5:19-23

The very first fruit that the Holy Spirit places in our hearts is LOVE. This is God's agape love, not natural, conditional love. All we have to do is draw this love out of our hearts by speaking the Word of God from a heart that believes God and loves Him, and He then can flood our whole being with the other fruit we need. I have done this in trying situations and found it really works.

A friend was sick and needed a ride to a medical clinic in another city. After waiting in the clinic with her for a while, I went out to the car to pray. I lifted my friend up to the throne of grace and asked for God's mercy for her in time of need (Heb. 4:16). She was in such pain and her face was very tense and miserable so I began praying the Word of God for her as I sat in the car. I began to draw the fruit of the Spirit out of the well of my spirit and I began to declare this fruit over her by quoting Galatians 5:22.

After a while I went inside and she was still sitting in the waiting room, but her face was so peaceful and filled with an awe and wonder. She asked me, "Were you just praying for me?" I told her I was and she said, "Something just came through that door and surrounded me and filled me with such peace and joy. I feel so much better!" We both knew it was the Holy Spirit Who had flooded God's love upon her to comfort her and healing had begun.

The Power of God's Compassion

I will never forget one example I had of the power of God's compassion to heal even those who had gone away from Him. I was the Prayer Partner Coordinator at TCT WAQP TV, and I was spending Saturday evening on the prayer phones praying for callers. When we are praying for callers on the prayer phones, the Lord will speak through us to encourage the faith of the callers to rise as they realize that the Lord has heard their cry and He loves them.

When the call came in I knew by the Spirit of God that it was very serious. The caller spoke in a very weak, slow and slurred voice as he told me that he was committing suicide by taking many drugs and didn't have long to live. He wanted me to pray that the Lord would forgive him and not send him to hell for killing himself. As prayer partner coordinator, I teach the prayer partners what to do if they have a suicide call, but let me tell you, when you get a call where the man has already taken the drugs and is almost dead, it can be very terrifying.

I cried out to God silently, asking Him what I should say to the man. I was alone and I knew there wasn't time to call anyone for help or try to get location information. Let me say here that it is very important when we are ministering to someone in desperate need, and any time actually, to be sure we are spiritually sensitive to hear the smallest whisper from the Holy Spirit as to what to say and do. Only the Lord knows the heart of the person in need.

In this case, the Holy Spirit didn't whisper, He spoke loudly and clearly, saying, ***"Pray for compassion!"*** That would have been surprising if I had taken time to think about it, because I thought I was there praying for people because of God's compassion.
I immediately prayed, "Lord! Give me your compassion!" And at that moment Compassion Himself hit me in the stomach so hard that I doubled over weeping and sobbing, in total loving compassion for the dying man. I have never known such love and compassion as I did then.

The man had been trying to explain in slurred dragged out words why he was killing himself and needed God to forgive him before he died. He said that he had been on drugs and had turned himself over to Teen Challenge to get himself clean.

He had won the victory and had overcome the drug addiction, however, when he got back home his old buddies had persuaded him to party with them and "try just one little hit, one won't hurt." He ended up back on drugs and Child Protective Services had to take his little four-year-old daughter away to a safe place. He was broken hearted and was weeping because he "had lost the only one in the world that loved me," he said.

I was weeping myself, but I managed to tell him that God loved him and I loved him. I truly expected him to scoff at the idea but instead he said in a tone of awe and wonder, "I feel that love!" I asked him if he could get his Bible and he managed to find it. I asked him to turn to Ephesians 3:14-21, the prayer Apostle Paul prayed for the church, and together the caller and I prayed on our knees the prayer concerning the awesome love of God that He downloads into our hearts that totally transforms us. Then I prayed for his healing, spirit, soul and body, and that the shalom of God would fill his heart to overflowing.

After I finished he spoke in a normal voice, in a tone of great joy and amazement. He said, "Sister! My high is gone!" We couldn't seem to stop praising the Lord for his healing and deliverance. I told him I would call Teen Challenge to see if they could help him with food and he said, "Okay, but not tonight. I need to go somewhere." He was just bubbling over with joy and excitement.

That was a Saturday night and the following Monday at work the prayer partner on duty called me at my desk and told me she had a wonderful testimony call. It was the suicidal man. He had checked himself into a hospital and he said they could find no trace of drugs in his system at all. That is a miracle! A miracle of God's loving compassion that not only heals our heart and soul, but also our body

Jesus taught that loving God and loving people is the most important rule of our lives and the Kingdom of God. We are the ones who must choose who we will obey, God's law of love or the law of our own selfish desires. We must never forget that the true meaning of sin is to miss the mark or take the wrong path. The devil's path always leads to destruction.

The suicidal man should have known better than to choose the wrong path after the training he received at Teen Challenge. I have known people that came through their program and they are taught the faith, hope and love that God gives us when we come to Him. But it is so vitally important that we find loving Christian friends to hang out with instead of the former friends who don't really care about us.

Jesus Will Never Leave Us

The devil tries to make us feel so alone and hopeless when we face trials of life. He plays on hurtful memories of past abandonment and rejection and magnifies them until they block the goodness of God's love for us. All we can do when feelings like that invade our minds is to stand on God's Word by meditating and speaking His promises until they change the darkness into God's light. I have done this many times.

> ***For He (God) Himself has said, I will not in any way fail you nor give you up nor leave you without support. (I will) not, (I will) not, (I will) not in any degree leave you helpless nor forsake nor let (you) down (relax My hold on you)! (Assuredly not)!***
>
> ***So we take comfort and are encouraged and confidently and boldly***

> ***say, The Lord is my Helper; I will not fear or dread or be terrified). What can man do to me?***
>
> ***Hebrews 13:5b-6 AMP***

It is so important that we believe God loves us and will never leave us or forsake us. We can learn the character of the Lord through the stories in the four gospels. Jesus healed and delivered everyone who came to Him and He said He only did what He saw His Father God do. When we see the loving character of Jesus we are seeing the love and character of our Father God. I have often thought how it must have hurt the heart of God to see His Son die such a terrible death, but He loved us so much He allowed Jesus to die so we could live with Him forever. The key to walking in God's promises is not to think we have to beg Him to help us but just to trust and believe that His Word is true and obey Him. If He said He loves us and will help us if we trust Him, then we can be sure that He will. We just have to ask and trust.

A Call to Witness

When I was at Beulah Heights Bible College in Atlanta, Georgia, my mom and dad became the cooks there to pay my way along with my little sister and brother. My life has always been filled with adventures, but some of my favorite adventures that fill me with awe of the Lord's faithfulness and love was during my second year at Bible College.

One of the most difficult classes that year was *Personal Evangelism.* The reason the class was difficult for me was because we were required to testify of the love of Jesus to a stranger every week or we would get a zero for that week. Let me tell you, I was horrified! I cried out to the Lord, "Lord! You know how shy I am. Please help me out of this terrible situation!" But guess what? I have discovered that the Lord will help me *through* the scary situations to teach me to rely on Him and trust His love instead of always helping me to run away in fear.

The Lord taught us in 1 John 4:18 that ***"Perfect love casts out fear."*** I learned this truth first hand as I started out to obey our teacher of *Personal Evangelism Class* to witness to strangers of the love of Jesus and His salvation. I asked the Lord to give me His compassion in my heart for people, to truly care about their salvation, not just to get a good grade. I also asked Him to bring to me the people that were ready to hear the Word of God and would receive the seed I would plant as the Holy Spirit spoke through me.

A lot of other students and I worked in department stores in Atlanta to help our parents pay for our schooling, and one of the most dramatic incidents of personal witnessing was the time a very dangerous man came to my counter where I worked.

It wasn't unusual to have a guy try to pick us up while we worked or were riding the bus but this particular guy had a very evil way about him. He began trying to get me to go with him when suddenly the spirit of the Lord came upon me very strongly and I started to declare the Word of God to him and warned him of hell fire, all in a much stronger way than I normally spoke to people. It was as though I couldn't stop my mouth and the words just poured out like a powerful river.

His face turned very red and then very pale and he almost ran out of the store. I heard people laughing and I turned and saw the store manager and another man watching me and they were doubled over laughing. I was immediately alarmed because Bible students were strictly warned never to preach to the customers or we would be fired.

The manager said to me, "What were you saying to that man?" I mumbled very low, "I preached at him," sure that I was now fired. I stared at them, shocked, as they started laughing again. The man standing with the manager told me that he was a detective and had been following and watching that man because girls were being kidnapped and harmed and they were certain he was the one but needed to catch him in the act. The detective said he had never seen anyone preach at the guy with such fervor and he had never seen him run like that from a girl. Of course, we know he wasn't running from me, he was running from God! I wasn't fired, thank God!

That class in Bible College became one of our favorite classes as we shared our experiences of witnessing for the Lord. It seemed as though the Lord searched for those who needed to hear the gospel and created a situation for each of the Bible students to witness for Him. Most situations the Lord sets up for us to witness will seem very ordinary and we need to walk close to the Lord so that we don't miss it.

For example, one night the manager sent another girl and I up to the attic to decorate chocolate Easter bunnies, and while we worked we got to know each other. When she found out I was a

Bible student she began to share sad situations in her life and had needed someone who would listen to her and pray with her. I know it was the Lord Who sent me up there and we ended up praying together as she gave her life back to the Lord.

One of the most amusing experiences was when I was sitting on a bus stop bench after work, very late at night, waiting for my bus. Suddenly two very smooth good-looking guys swooped down, one on each side of me. One started his spiel by saying, "We're from the Holy Land and we would really like to get to know you…" Before he could continue I said, "Oh how wonderful! Then you must know Jesus the Messiah. He came down from Heaven to the Holy Land to die on the cross to save us and He loves us all so much!"

I went on and on without stopping as they stared at me, as fascinated as a deer in headlights. After a while they tore their eyes away and shared a look that said, "We have got to get away from here!" One of them told me it was nice meeting me but they really had to go. After they were gone I laughed, but I prayed that the seed that was planted in them would grow up and they would accept Jesus as their Messiah.

The Holy Spirit that lives in our spirit is not at all shy and fearful. Our soul is the seat of our emotions, and the past events of our lives cause many emotions that can hinder us from walking with the Lord. Fear is like a demon that has us chained to the fearful memory, stopping us from going forward in faith to obey the Lord. So, how can we overcome our fears and walk in faith?

We must always keep in the forefront of our thoughts that the powerful weapon of the spoken Word of God is only empowered by our faith in God, and that faith only works by love, the first fruit of the Holy Spirit in our spirit. So we are not without the weapons we need to win.

> ***For the Word of God is living and powerful, and sharper than any two-edged sword, piercing even to the division of soul and spirit, and of joints and marrow, and is a discerner of the thoughts and intents of the heart. And there is no creature hidden from His sight, but all things are naked and open to the eyes of Him to whom we must give account.***
>
> ***Seeing then that we have a great High Priest Who has passed through the heavens, Jesus the Son of God, let us hold fast our confession.***
>
> ***For we do not have a High Priest Who cannot sympathize with our weaknesses, but in all points tempted as we are, yet without sin.***
>
> ***Let us therefore come boldly to the throne of grace, that we may obtain mercy and find grace to help in time of need.***
>
> ***Hebrews 4:12-16 NKJV***

Years ago when I lived in Tulsa, I began my prayers for others with Hebrews 4:16, bringing them in confidence (boldly) to the Lord at His throne of grace. When I came back to Michigan, an evangelist at a church service had a word for me from the Lord, saying, "When you pray for people, you bring them before My throne of grace.

Those who you bring before My throne of grace will receive the request that you ask when they choose to believe." Since love causes believing faith to work, we can see why the first fruit of the Holy Spirit is so important. I knew that word the evangelist gave was truly from the Lord because I had never told anyone that I began my payers for people this way, and I could sense the Presence of the Lord so powerfully.

How do we obtain and daily live in this powerful love that empowers our faith to overcome trouble? By choosing every morning to set aside a special time and place to worship the Lord from the bottom of our hearts. I asked the Lord to wake me up an hour earlier than necessary to get ready for work and that was my special time with Him. It became such a glorious and intimate prayer time that I have never wanted to miss it for any reason. That special prayer time in the "secret place of the Most High" (see Psalm 91:1) has expanded to most of the morning.

It is in this secret place of the Most High that the strength and courage that comes from the Lord is downloaded into out spirits. Then we can pray for others with God's faith, love and power to change their lives as well as ours. Not too long ago I went to the hospital to pray for someone who was facing surgery for cancer. As I anointed him with oil on his forehead and then laid my hands on his arm as I prayed, I felt absolutely nothing. Normally I feel a strong surge of the Holy Spirit as I pray. I simply prayed the Word of God in faith for his healing and stood in faith that the Lord heard my prayer and answered.

As I looked at him I saw tears in his eyes and he said he had never before felt such a strong surge of the power of the Holy Spirit on his forehead and arm as he touched the cancer mass. I asked him if it was like a warmth and he said, "No, it was like a surge of electricity and an overwhelming love of the Lord." I knew he had been preparing his spirit by meditating on the Word of God and worshipping the Lord. He was ready to receive from God because meditating the Word of God allows the Holy Spirit to cause our faith to grow and He imparts the love of God into our spirit. When we know beyond a shadow of doubt that God really does love us, we are able to believe for His salvation, healing and deliverance.

Meditation in God's Word is the key, reading it out loud concerning the problem we are dealing with and applying it to our lives. But just reading the Bible without knowing Jesus personally is like trying turn on a lamp that isn't plugged into electricity. Electricity is there waiting, the lamp plug is there, but we are the one that has to plug it in. Many years ago, when I was first learning the ways of the Lord, I asked Him to help me understand what His power and presence was like. I needed a mental picture. He spoke a word to me in my heart that I heard very clearly, He said, "electricity." A million thoughts raced through my mind concerning electricity. The same power that turns on a lamp and brings light in a dark place, will also cool a refrigerator to keep food from spoiling, heat a burner to cook food so we can eat, and on and on.

So, how do we plug into this glorious power of God? I believe It begins by "seeking His Face", to know Him first as our Savior, then to start on the awesome journey to know Him personally as our friend as well as Lord and King of our lives.

On any journey, we have free will to choose the way we will go. There will be times in our lives when we come to a crossroad and we have to make a choice. Jesus loves us so much and He wants a close relationship and intimate fellowship with us, but as He stands at the crossroads waiting for our decision, He will never force us to choose His way. If we haven't heard His still small voice in a long time, we need to check to see if we have taken the wrong path, thought and spoken hurtful, blaming words toward Him, ***and gone our own way.***

He is waiting for us to repent and come back to the Shepherd of our souls. To repent means to realize we have gone the wrong way, ask forgiveness, and turn around and go the right way. This fills Jesus' heart with such joy. He told a minister that as much as it hurts Him when we stumble and fall, it fills Him with way more joy when we get back up and start walking with Him again.

Each person has their own special time that they set aside for intimate fellowship with the Lord. I have wonderful times of worship in His Presence when I am driving and I am singing with worship music, just loving on Him. But my most special time is very early in the morning when I am alone with God in my "secret place of the Most High." Psalm 91:1.

If we get too busy or are too upset and angry to repent and turn back to God, we may start to neglect those special times alone with God. If this happens, our hearts can grow cold and callous toward Him and toward others and we could find that we have left our first love. A fearful, angry cold heart hurts the heart of the One who loves us so dearly and it also hurts our heart, soul and body as well.

Jesus talked about this in Revelation 2:3-5 when He appeared to John in the Isle of Patmos during great persecution of the church under Nero and later under Domitian.

> ***I know all the things you do. I have seen your hard work and your patient endurance. I know you don't tolerate evil people. You have examined the claims of those who say they are apostles but are not.***

> ***You have discovered they are liars. You have patiently suffered for me without quitting.***
>
> ***But I have this complaint against you. You don't love Me or each other as you did at first. Look how far you have fallen! Turn back to Me and do the works you did at first. If you don't repent I will come and remove your lamp stand from its place among the churches.***

This is the way King James Version puts it:

> ***Nevertheless, I have this against you, that you have left your first love.***

If we have left our first love through neglect of our special time alone with Jesus and our hearts have become cold and hard, we may not realize it at first and the Lord has to get our attention. If we never have time to go on a date with our friends or spouse, a distance will grow between you and love will grow cold. If your friend really loves you they will try to get your attention to try to regain the lost love. Maybe a wife will stop talking to her husband and he will notice and ask her, "Honey, what's wrong?" That will open the door of communication again so she can ask him for a special time alone with just the two of them to regain their special love.

I do believe that sometimes prayer is not answered immedi-ately because the Lord has His own timetable for His own reasons. The Lord will give a miracle at times, but a lot of times it seems as though He likes to heal or deliver through a process. The condition of our hearts may need as much healing as the problem we are facing, and He knows that may take time alone with Him. Why would that be? One reason could be the strongholds in our minds have to come down. This takes more than just a different thought to cast out another thought that is wrong. If we grew up believing we are unlovable, or bad, for example, just saying over and over that we are worthy of love and a good person will help some, but that would take a really long time.

We need the Word of God, the Name of Jesus and the blood of the Lamb of God to tear down those strongholds that have been there for a long time and heal the wounded heart. We should never buy into the old phrase, “Well, we’re only human, I just can’t change the way I was made.” We are made in the image and likeness of God. He created us to love and be loved. We are the way we are because of what we choose to think and believe.

CHAPTER FOUR

THE PATH OF LIFE

> ***But I did find this: God created people to be virtuous, but they have each turned to follow their own downward path.***
>
> ***Ecclesiastes 7:29***

We face many hard situations and even persecutions in life, but we do not need to give in and run and hide. What can we do when we face an enemy or something bigger than we are? It was more than a small stone that brought down Goliath. It was the words of faith in his blood covenant with God that David spoke from his heart to Goliath that put the power of God behind that stone. David knew his God. Look at 1 Samuel 17:45-47

> ***You come to me with sword, spear, and javelin, but I come to you in the Name of the Lord of Heaven's Armies-the God of the armies of Israel, whom, you have defied. Today the Lord will conquer you, and I will kill you and cut off your head….and the whole world will know that there is a God in Israel. And everyone assembled here will know that the Lord rescues His people, but not with sword and spear. This is the Lord's battle, and He will give you to us!"***

I believe that sometimes we face a Goliath for the sake of others, like David. The Lord sent David to Israel's army deliberately to bring down Goliath. I have been in uncomfortable and dangerous situations that were not of my own making and realized later that there was a reason for it. The Lord always delivered me just in time as I spoke His word in prayer, or just plain cried out "Jesus save me!"

It is always so amazing to see the enemy back off at the name of Jesus and the Word of God spoken in faith.

Hebrews 4:12 tells us that it is God's Word that is so sharp and powerful that it can divide between our soul with all its fearful memories and the spirit of man, which is the abiding place of the Holy Spirit when we are born again. How can mere words on a page be so powerful? Because the Word of God is not just mere words on a page. They are God's words, and they are in fact alive with the power of the Holy Spirit just as Hebrews 4:12 states.

One young lady I know found herself on the wrong path when she ran away from home with her boyfriend. She ended up in a terrifying situation with a group of evil men and she ran from the house, out into the darkness. She felt so lost and alone because her boyfriend was angry when she refused to do the evil things he wanted and she found herself abandoned in another state from her home.

As she walked in the darkness, not knowing where to go and having no money, she began to pray for God to forgive her and help her. Suddenly she heard some men calling out evil things to her and they began to come after her. As she ran the men chased her, calling out the things they were going to do to her and she remembered that her mother had taught her to speak the Word of God when she was in danger. She was so frightened that all she could think of was simple verses such as, "The Lord is my shepherd!" and "Jesus saves!" She spoke these words as she ran and suddenly the footsteps that had been getting closer and closer suddenly were gone. I am sure the angels "hearkened to the Word of the Lord" and chased the men away.

Her mother had been praying for her return and was very concerned because she was moving to another state and didn't know where her daughter was. Her daughter would come home to an empty house and not know where her family had gone.

Then, just a few days before her mother moved, an evangelist she had never met before gave her a word from the Lord at a Women Aglow meeting. The evangelist said that morning before the meeting the Lord told her there would be a mother there whose teenage daughter had run away and was in trouble. The evangelist came over to where the mother was sitting and gave her the message from the Lord.

The Lord said that He would speak to the teen to call and when the mother goes to get her from the other state, do not rebuke or scold her, say only loving and kind words. He told the mother to treat her like a princess because He loves her very much. It happened just as the Lord had spoken. God is so good!

Even though we get on the wrong path, when we cry out to the Lord for help and repent, He will wash away our sin and rescue us from the wrong path and bring us onto the path of righteousness.

> ***The Lord is my shepherd; I shall not want.***
>
> ***He makes me to lie down in green pastures; He leads me beside the still waters.***
>
> ***He restores my soul. He leads me in the paths of righteousness for His name's sake.***

> ***Yea, though I walk through the valley of the shadow of death, I will fear no evil; for You are with me; Your rod and Your staff; they comfort me.***
>
> ***You prepare a table before me in the presence of my enemies; you anoint my head with oil; my cup runs over.***
>
> ***Surely goodness and mercy shall follow me all the days of my life; and I will dwell in the house of the Lord forever.***
>
> ***Psalm 23***

When the Word of God is so strong in our hearts that it is part of us, it will be a weapon that we can and must use against the enemy of our souls. Jesus gave us full armor for protection and also to fight against the devils that try to ensnare and destroy us.

> ***Finally, my brethren, be strong in the Lord and in the power of His might.***
>
> ***Put on the whole armor of God that you may be able to stand against the wiles (evil tricks) of the devil.***
>
> ***Eph. 6:10-13 NKJV***

Kidnapped

When I was younger, I continued living in Atlanta, Georgia in the Bible College apartments for a period of time after I graduated. Since I didn't have a car I had to walk seven blocks to the bus stop or take a taxi to work. I generally walked to the bus stop since I was quite frugal with my money so I could spend it on clothes. (Smile) One morning I stood at the window looking at the driving rain that was pouring down, dreading the walk to the bus stop. I thought about the nice old man that ran a small store on the corner who had always been friendly to the students and sometimes asked us if he could give us a ride. We always declined, but this morning I decided that I would accept if he came by.

I had my huge umbrella shielding my face and shoulders and I walked quickly toward the bus stop, hoping I wouldn't have sopping wet shoes all day. Then I saw the white car, just like the one the nice old man drove. It stopped by me and he motioned me to come to the other side of the car and get in. I was so thankful! I ran quickly around the back of the car and he opened the door from his driver's side. I bent down to smile and speak to him to thank him when I saw with a shock that the man was a stranger that looked like the old man. I began to back away, saying, "I'm sorry, I thought you were someone else..." That was all I had time to say because he grabbed my arm and roughly jerked me into the car. I tried to pull away but he stomped on the gas and drove quickly down the street.

I was still trying to be polite and explain that I didn't know him and he had made a mistake, would he please stop the car and let me out. Then his evil nature came out and he began to yell at me, trying to intimidate me, saying things like, "We may not know each other now but we will as soon as I get you to Florida!"

He then started to tell me what he was going to do to me in Florida, but he wouldn't hurt me if I would just be quiet and let him do what he wanted to do. He said I was in his control now and had no choice but to go quietly if I wanted to come out of it "in one piece." Words like that.

At first I was so shocked that I was just paralyzed with fear. I couldn't believe it was really happening to me. Somehow, I think we unconsciously believe evil will never touch us, and we will just smooth right along in life, praying for other people when they are attacked, but we ourselves are immune. I simply cried out, "Jesus, help me!" Not a long scripture filled prayer, but one right from the heart.

Suddenly I was no longer the paralyzed rabbit, I became a different woman! The Spirit of the Lord arose in me like a lion and I was in his face, yelling at him louder than he was yelling at me. I heard scriptures pouring out of my mouth that I had memorized for Personal Evangelism class but thought I had probably forgotten. I preached at him like the most powerful evangelist you ever heard. I don't remember everything I said but it was almost all scripture.

There is one thing I do remember saying. I said, "Your mother is in heaven right now watching you and she is so ashamed of you!" As soon as it came out of my mouth I wondered why I had said it. I didn't know him or his mother. Amazingly, he stopped yelling and became quiet. I kept on talking in a quiet voice about the love of the Lord and the power of the Word of God and that Jesus came to save us even though we have all been evil and selfish in our hearts.

Then as he came to an exit on the expressway he pulled off and began to cross over the expressway to the north bound entrance. I asked him, "Where are you going now?" He replied, "I'm taking you back, Lady!" I said, "Well, you have made me late for work so I need you to take me there."

All the way back to Atlanta I kept talking, in a normal tone of voice, about Jesus and how He can change our lives by washing away our sin and heal the wounds in our hearts. He never said a word the whole way back to my job. When he stopped in front of the telephone company where I worked and I got out he finally spoke. He said, "Lady, be more careful next time." I said, "I will. And don't you forget the things I have told you." He replied, "I won't!"

As I walked toward the big glass doors of the telephone company I suddenly became as weak as a wet noodle. I could hardly get the front doors open. I looked back at the man as he sat there looking at me and I started to get scared that he would jump out of the car and grab me again. I realized how powerful the anointing of the Holy Spirit is because when that special anointing lifted I became, for a minute, a scared rabbit again. However, I threw that off really quick and reminded myself that if he did try to get me again I could just call on Jesus and He would save me.

As I got to my position at work the girl next to me said, "Where have you been?" Then she saw my face and said, "What happened? Your face is white as a sheet!" I told her that I had been kidnapped and Jesus had rescued me. Talk about an opening to tell about Jesus and His love for us! I have thought many times about the whole incident and I realize it was the Word of God and His Holy Spirit dwelling in me that saved me.

I have prayed for that man that the seed of the Word of God would grow in his heart and he would accept Jesus as Lord and Savior. I prayed that he would study the Word of God and I know the Word of God in his heart would then begin to renew his mind and transform him from a rapist to a servant of the Most High God.

The Wrong Mentality

When we read in the Bible about the Children of Israel in the wilderness and how the Lord rescued them from Egypt, then had to spend forty years trying to get the Egypt victim-slavery mentality out of them, we begin to understand how the things that have happened to us can affect us. It should have only taken them forty days to get across the wilderness and enter their promised land but instead it took them forty years. Mainly, like us sometimes, they kept their focus on themselves and their difficulties instead of their loving and powerful God.

Unfortunately, the abuse in our young lives can give us this victim-slave mentality, as I mentioned in an earlier chapter. We wonder what on earth makes us act the way we do sometimes. Jesus said that we judge and blame other people for their self-centered complaining and cruel words and actions when all the time we do the same thing. We can see it in others but it's not as easy to see it in ourselves.

I believe the man who kidnapped me suddenly saw himself as he really was when, by the Spirit of God, I mentioned his mother watching him. He seemed to suddenly be shocked into silence.

Hurting People Hurt People

I have thought about him over the years and wondered what makes a person turn into such an abusive, hurtful, dangerous character. I will never know his life story, but I do know that hurting people hurt other people.

I saw a newscast once that I will never forget. It was a live feed of the aftermath of a deadly gang war. There were policemen everywhere and young people were lying on the ground, wounded, possibly some dead, with ambulances there and paramedics working with the wounded.

The reporter on TV was interviewing a young gang member who had survived and was asking him why he would take part in such a bloody violent action. I will never forget the young man's eyes as he answered. They were so bleak and sad as he looked into the camera and said, "Man, I hurt so bad myself on the inside that it makes me feel better to hurt someone else." I could feel his pain and I cried the tears he couldn't seem to cry. I prayed God's mercy for him and the other young people whose lives had been so shattered and broken.

Destructive pain like that usually comes from feeling betrayed and unloved, which produces rage and anger. I wanted to run to where he and the other young people were and tell them that there was One, the Lamb of God, Who loved them unconditionally, no matter what sin they had committed, and He would forgive them and never betray and abandon them.

I wanted to tell them that sin is "missing the mark" and "taking the wrong path" by Hebrew definition, but Jesus is waiting and longing to go after them and bring them back to His path. If they only truly knew His path was a path of light, life and love, they would not be afraid to walk with Him.

> ***You will show me the path of life; in Your presence is fullness of joy. At your right hand there are pleasures forevermore.***
>
> ***Psalm 16:11***

A wonderful evangelist and teacher on TV told a story about Jesus going after the lost sheep that really touched me. He said he was in his bathroom shaving and said to Jesus, "Jesus, I love you." Suddenly the Lord replied out loud (to him) and said, "How much?" The evangelist was shocked and said, "Well, a lot!" Jesus asked, "More than the least of these?" (See Matthew 25:40) The evangelist said, "Yes". Jesus replied, "So, who do you consider least?"

He stopped for a minute and thought about people who had turned against him and spoken evil of him unjustly, but he didn't want to say that to Jesus. Of course, Jesus knows our thoughts and He replied, "Well, they are not least to Me. I came after you when you were wrong and deceived in many ways and I am going after them. Will you go with Me?"

When I heard that I began to weep and I told the Lord, "I want to go with You too. I want to walk close behind you when you go after the lost sheep and lost lambs. Help me to walk in your footsteps and not go down a wrong path or fall in a ditch somewhere. With all my heart I want to bring people to You for cleansing, healing and deliverance." This is the greatest desire of

my heart.
I believe this is the desire of all of us. We see wounded and broken people everywhere and we ask the Lord for opportunities to tell them that the Good Shepherd, Jesus, is searching for them because He loves them and His deepest desire is to rescue and heal them. The problem is, how do we get them to listen with their hearts and not just argue that God simply cannot be real or good or strong since there is so much pain and destruction in this world?

One of the devil's favorite tricks to lure them away from the loving Shepherd, Jesus, is through the deep-seated pain of rejection. Jesus understands that pain because the Bible says He suffered rejection for us so we could be accepted and loved by His Father God.

> ***Who has believed our message? To whom has the LORD revealed His powerful arm? My servant grew up in the LORD'S presence like a tender green shoot, like a root in dry ground.***
>
> ***There was nothing beautiful or majestic about His appearance, nothing to attract us to Him. He was despised and rejected-a man of sorrows, acquainted with deepest grief. We turned our backs on Him and looked the other way. He was despised, and we did not care.***
>
> ***Yet it was our weaknesses His carried; it was our sorrows that weighed Him down. And we thought His troubles were a punishment from God, a punishment for His own sins! But He was pierced for our rebellion, crushed for our sins. He was beaten so we could be whole. He was whipped so we could be healed. All of us, like sheep, have strayed away. We have left God's paths to follow our own. Yet the LORD laid on Him the sins of us all.***
>
> ***Isaiah 53:1-7***

The devil will cause people to ignore or even mock us so that we will be intimidated and fear rejection. God created each of us with the desire for fellowship with friends because that is His nature and desire also. We were created in His image and likeness, to be like Him, and it gives Him pain when we are rejected and ignored. And I am sure it hurts Him when we reject other people.

Jesus said that the things we do to the least of His brethren, "You did it unto Me." Psychologists say that the abuse of speaking hurtful mean words and yelling at your family and friends is more hurtful and damaging than actual physical abuse.

Many people say that they stopped attending church because they were so hurt by self-righteous judgmental Christians. Unfortunately, this has happened all too often. What we don't realize is that some of these hurtful condemning religious people are wounded and hurting themselves and are just covering it up instead of taking their pain to Jesus to let Him heal them. They may be afraid to admit to not being perfect, lest they be rejected themselves. So they mouth the religious words of the Bible, but the power and glory of God's Word has never really entered their hearts to transform them. Some may say they are Christians but were never actually saved.

He Heals the Wounded Heart

When younger, I had been very wounded by rejection and began to attend a class for wounded people taught by a wonderful Christian psychologist. She would take seven wounded ladies into her home once a week and charge us very little to teach and disciple us in the Word and love of the Lord. I have never forgotten the very first class. We were all very shy and quiet, not wanting to draw attention to ourselves, lest we be rejected as not perfect enough for acceptance.

After she had taught us about God's love for us, and made sure we had all accepted Jesus as savior, she asked us if we believed Jesus was telling the truth that Father God loved us so much that He sent Jesus to die for us. Of course, we said, "Yes." Then she said that if we believed we were truly loved by God we would do as Jesus did and minister to one another.

We were stunned. I glanced around and everyone had the same shocked and unbelieving look on their faces, thinking, "What do you mean, minister and pray for someone else? I can scarcely pray for myself!" She saw the stunned look on our faces and probably wanted to laugh but she was compassionate. She told us to pair up with another person that we didn't know and pray for them, and if we couldn't pray, just say, "God bless you."

I was sitting beside a girl I didn't know and she was even more quiet and shy than I was. I'm sure she was thinking the same thing I was; "This is never going to work. I can't do this!" We took each other's hands and after a short silence I asked her if she wanted to go first. After a minute, she whispered, very low, "God bless you."

Then it was my turn. I was used to praying by going before the throne of God's grace, as I had learned in Bible College, and as I did I would always be filled with the love of God. So this is what I did, lifting her up before the throne of God, and in my imagination we were kneeling before Him, thanking Him for His love and salvation. All I said out loud was something like this, "Father God, I come before your throne of grace in the Name of Jesus and I am asking for your mercy. I ask You to please pour Your Light, Life and Love into her heart tonight. Thank you. We love you." That was the extent of my prayer.

We all continued to attend those classes for several years and I learned that the girl I had prayed for had been so horribly abused and molested by a family member that she was traumatized and never spoke very much. After my last class there just before I left for Michigan she came out to my car as I was about to drive away and very softly whispered to me, "You have the gift of gentleness. When you prayed for me that first day, I saw a shaft of bright light come from the throne of God and pierce through the wall of ice I had around my heart. I felt the love of God flood my heart in such a strong way and I knew my healing had started." I was so amazed. I had no idea that had happened, although I had seen her begin to change over the years we attended the class.

This is what the Lord can do through us even when we are still wounded ourselves. In a war, wounded people help other wounded people all the time. As we pray for others, we ourselves are healed. I have seen it happen many times through the years.

Jan Crouch from TBN tells her story of receiving her healing from emotional illness as compassion filled her heart for a young lady weeping at an altar. The Lord told her to go to the young lady and pray for her. Jan said she hesitated at first because she felt she was so wounded herself she couldn't possible minister to anyone else. She finally obeyed the Lord and as the compassion of the Lord poured through her for the young lady, her own healing began.

I do need to say one thing, the Lord had specifically told Jan to minister to her and we have to truly be led by the Lord to do this. Sometimes wounded people are so focused on their own pain that they don't really know the Lord in a personal intimate way and do not have His love in their heart. They can do great harm to others with hurtful words.

The Lord spoke to my heart once when I was studying for a Bible class, saying that the sword of the Spirit, the Word of God, must be wielded very carefully. We must always be as gentle and careful as a surgeon removing a cancer, and never as an assassin. That Christian psychologist told us at the beginning of the class that if we continued studying with her we could eventually rise until we would be able to teach the class ourselves. I studied with her for years, until I left Tulsa.

The Lord had spoken to my heart and told me I was in the process of receiving my healing and would teach again and I would be teaching wounded women. This was difficult to believe even though I had been a teacher for years, even teaching the teenage Sunday School class when I was a teenager myself.

When I got to Michigan the Lord continued to speak to my heart and He spoke to me through prophetic people that healing and deliverance was in my hands and in His Word, that I would teach.

I was to love and disciple those who had wandered away from Him. I believe the Lord downloaded His compassion into me and that is probably why I weep whenever I see wounded people like the young man in that gang war. However, we know that having compassion for people isn't going to help them if we don't pray for them and ask the Lord for the opportunity to minister to them.

We must tell them that Jesus loved them so much that He suffered horrible beatings and died on a cross, shedding His blood to cleanse their sin, heal and deliver them from the kingdom of Satan.

Healing a Wounded Soul

Most of the people I talk and pray with have suffered great sorrows, leaving great wounds in their soul. If these wounds are untreated by the blood of the Lamb of God, they can cause various spiritual infections. I guess that sounds weird, but that is what the Lord showed me in a vision concerning my own soul.

About thirty years ago, I moved into a house that, I believe, had residing demons in it. The first Sunday after I moved in I woke up in suicidal depression and the first thought that came to me was to find a way to kill myself. It felt like I was encased in an ice straitjacket. I could barely get out of bed to get ready for church. It was a step by step process and I had to tell myself each step to take. The next day I was fine and could go to work with no problem. Then when Sunday came I went through it all over again. I never told anyone. But the Lord knew. I just kept crying out to Him for help and grace and commanded that demon of depression to go, and it would, until the next Sunday. This made no sense to me.

One Sunday morning our church had a guest speaker from England that I had never met and who was powerful in the gifts of the Spirit. After the message he was laying hands on the sick and speaking words of knowledge to the people who came for prayer. He spoke to me as I sat in my seat and said, "You are dealing with a suicidal depression spirit and if you will come up here for prayer the Lord will deliver you." I went forward for prayer and he cast that evil spirit off me and I was filled with such joy and peace.

This lasted for many months until one Sunday I woke up with that suicidal depression over me again. I was so angry! How dare that devil come back to torment me after he had been cast off me!

Looking back, I believe he had a right to come back because I had just gone through a very painful rejection and betrayal by a close friend and my thoughts were not very loving and peaceful. If I had loved her, forgiven her and prayed for her as I knew I should have, it never could have come to torment me. As soon as I got back from church that day I spent the next three hours on my face on the floor before God asking Him for understanding and wisdom as to why that devil thought he had a right to come and torment me.

Suddenly I had a vision from the Lord. I saw my heart, not the blood pump but it was more like the core of my being. I saw a deep wound and there was infection in the wound. I asked the Lord, "What is that infection?" The Lord answered me, "Pride and rejection." I was amazed. How could pride and rejection both be the cause of such infection in a wounded heart?

I asked the Lord, "Will you cleanse it out for me? I can't do it by myself." He reached down and cleansed the wound and bandaged it with such wonderful love and compassion. I began to heal rapidly from that moment. I never had depression like that again. I have spent the last thirty years with a "dancing heart that brings me joy and happiness." That was told to me just recently by a wonderful evangelist and author who did not know me, and it was true.

Words are Powerful!

There is something else I need to say here. Someone wanted to pray for me over the phone and I allowed them to do so. In the prayer, he made the statement to the Lord that I had been depressed for the last ten years. Someone must have told him that because it was not the truth, however I let it stand without saying anything, out of courtesy. Huge mistake! I woke up the next morning in deep depression, but not suicidal.

I immediately commanded the devil to leave me, and he did. But several times over the next few weeks, depression would suddenly hit me, even sitting in church. It was always after a thought of being rejected would enter my mind. I fought both the thoughts and the depression with the Word of God as Jesus did in the wilderness temptation in Luke 4:1-13.

I asked the Lord, "Lord, am I going to have to fight this for the rest of my life?" After church one Sunday night a powerful apostle, prophet and pastor told me the Lord would fight for me with His sword, which I knew to be the Word of God. I was filled with such joy and from that day on I have never had a bit of depression and I am continually filled with the joy of the Lord and His peace again.

I believe I should have corrected the person who prayed over the phone for me when he said that I had been depressed for the last ten years. It is possible to correct someone with respect and honor without being offensive, and we simply cannot let a wrong statement about us go like that.

The Power of Thoughts and Words

All of this just to say that our thoughts and words are very powerful things. They can take us down the wrong path if they are fearful, negative and angry, or they can put us on the right path if our thoughts are filled with faith in God and His Word.

We also need to be very sensitive to the leading of the Holy Spirit because our words can be very hurtful to someone else, or they can lift a person up and give them new strength and courage in the battles of life. We must never speak impulsively out of our soulish fleshly realm to someone concerning their life. I heard a well-known evangelist say on TV that the Lord told him to pray for people to be healed from the wounding of negative and hurtful words that had been spoken to them. As soon as he said that I knew it was true.

Effective and fervent prayer is very necessary before we speak into someone's life about something negative that needs to be corrected. We have to know beyond a shadow of doubt that the Lord has directed the words we speak to them and He has filled our hearts and words with His truth and love.

Jesus is our example and He told us to take up our cross and follow Him if we want to be His disciple. That means we don't just do and say anything we want to anymore. He only did and said what His Father in heaven taught Him to say.

> ***He who sent Me is true and I speak to the world those things which I heard from Him.***
>
> ***John 8:26b***

> ***When you lift up the Son of Man, then you will know that I am He, and I do nothing of Myself, but as My Father taught Me, I do these things.***

> ***And He Who sent Me is with Me. The Father has not left Me alone, for I always do those things that please Him.***
>
> ***John 8:28-29 NKJV***

Jesus spent many hours alone praying to His Father, usually at night. Then, during the day, He walked with His Father God and said and did only what His Father told Him to say and do.

Jesus had emotions just like we do, after all we are created in His image and likeness. However, He never allowed Himself to react to the mean things that unbelievers said and did to Him. We can't just excuse ourselves by thinking, "Well, I can't help it! They are so mean, I just had to let them have it!"

If we give in to the angry emotions we may ask the Lord to forgive us, but then the next time we give in to "letting they have it" again. Then it becomes a pattern in our mind and a path or track in our brain to always react with anger in retaliation to abuse.

The Holy Spirit will speak to our hearts and counsel us to be still and seek the wisdom of the Lord before we react and speak. At the same time our own thoughts or even the thoughts of the devil are whispering in our ear to speak wrong words when hurtful words are spoken to us. We must choose whose words we will believe and obey.

I grew up listening and learning from Oral Roberts, and one day he said that the Lord spoke to him and gave him wisdom for difficult situations. The Lord said to him: "There is always a key issue that you won't perceive without God's light, wisdom and faith."

He went on to say that we need to stop and decide whose words we are going to listen to. Whose mind-set and attitude is framing our way of thinking. Words cause images and ideas that create the right or wrong intent of our heart. He said we should always step back and judge the intent of our heart; is it selfish, self-promoting or self-protecting? Or is Jesus the King of our heart? I know from dealing with hurting people, listening to the agony of their mind and heart and helping them to reach out in faith to the Lord as we pray, that some hurts are very deep.

People who were abused as a child very often become like the abusive parent or the abusive person who tried to control them and manipulate them through fear. Why would this happen? It's through unforgiving thought patterns they have developed over the years that were ingrained in their brain by speaking the wrong words, to themselves or out loud.

Not forgiving those who abused you is usually based on fear and can actually cause your mind and eventually your brain to be damaged or warped. The world says our brain controls our mind, but the Lord is saying we can choose to think right thoughts with the help of the Holy Spirit and those right thoughts will change our brain. Science has now proven this.

What did Jesus teach us about thinking fearful angry thoughts or thoughts of worry and hopelessness?

> ***Therefore take no thought saying, what shall we eat? Or, what shall we drink? Or, wherewithal shall we be clothed?***
>
> ***For after all these things do the Gentiles seek: for your Heavenly Father knoweth that ye have need of all these things.***
>
> ***But seek ye first the kingdom of God and His righteousness; and all these things shall be added unto you.***
>
> *Matthew 6:31-34 KJV*

Jesus told us to "take no thought, saying", which means we take the thought by saying it. So if we choose to cast out our fearful worried thoughts and begin speaking the Word of God from a heart that trusts God, we can overcome wrong thoughts.

CHAPTER FIVE

HOW ABOUT YOUR HEART?

What happens to a heart that is deeply wounded and the person doesn't cast out the hurtful words and angry thoughts that come? If we continue to meditate on the offense instead of choosing to forgive and love, we harden our hearts. Then the Word of God cannot sink deep into our hearts and grow up to bear much fruit. This is how Jesus taught about our hearts, they are the soil where He plants His seed, the Word of God.

> ***A farmer went out to plant his seed. As he scattered it across his field, some seed fell on a footpath, where it was stepped on and the birds ate it.***
>
> ***Other seed fell among rocks. It began to grow but the plant soon wilted and died for lack of moisture. Other seed fell among thorns that grew up with it and choked out the tender plants. Still other seed fell on fertile soil.***
>
> ***This seed grew and produced a crop that was a hundred times as much as had been planted. When He had said this he called out, "Anyone with ears to hear should listen and understand."***
>
> ***Luke 8:5-8***
>
> ***This is the meaning of the parable. The seed is God's Word. The seeds that fell on the footpath represent those who hear the message, only to have the devil come and take it away from their hearts and prevent them from believing and being saved.***

> ***The seeds on the rocky soil represent those who hear the message and receive it with joy, but since they don't have deep roots, they believe for a while, then they fall away when they face temptations.***
>
> ***The seeds that fell among the thorns represent those who hear the message but all too quickly the message is crowded out by the cares and riches and pleasures of this life.***
>
> ***And so they never grow into maturity. And the seeds that fell on the good soil represent honest, good-hearted people who hear God's Word, cling to it, and patiently produce a huge harvest.***
>
> ***Luke 8:11-15***

Look how Matthew explains the parable Jesus told.

> ***Now listen to the explanation of the parable about the farmer planting seeds. The seed that fell on the footpath represents those who hear the message about the kingdom and don't understand it. Then the evil one comes and snatches away the seed that was planted in their hearts. The seed on the rocky soil represents those who hear the message and immediately receive it with joy. But since they don't have deep roots, they don't last long. They fall away as soon as they have problems or are persecuted for believing God's Word. The seed that fell among the thorns represents those who hear God's Word but all too quickly the message is crowded out by the worries of this life and the lure of wealth, so no fruit is produced. The seed that fell on good soil represents those who truly hear and understand God's Word and produce a harvest of thirty, sixty or even a hundred times as much as had been planted.***
>
> ***Matthew 13:16-23***

As I read this passage several years ago, I was very impacted by something I believe the Lord showed me about the seed that fell on the footpath. The birds could easily snatch up the seed and eat it because the ground had been hardened by people walking on it and the seed couldn't enter in and begin to grow roots. He showed me that the reason people can't seem to comprehend the love of God and the awesome plan He has for their lives is because their hearts have become hard from the hurts of their past.

For example, a heart that is hardened to their earthly father will find it very difficult to receive the blessing of their heavenly Father. In their mind they know it wasn't their heavenly Father who hurt them, still, in their heart they can't help but think that God could have fixed the situation and made their earthly father love them, bless them and treat them with respect.

It is so important for our lives that we receive the blessing of our fathers. I have watched people struggle all their lives because they were ignored and abused by their parents. How can we receive the blessing of our natural father and mother if they are not willing to bless us or are gone? Rather than just harden our hearts to the pain of rejection from our natural fathers, we can turn to our Father in heaven and receive His loving acceptance and blessing.

I was impacted by a powerful man of God who was teaching on having a heart of love for God and people in order to be a true prayer intercessor. He shared his testimony of his struggles as a pastor many years ago because of hurtful wounds in his heart that had not been healed. He was an awesome teacher and preacher (I know because I heard him teach) but he seemed to have trouble becoming close to the people in his church, even though he loved them.

One day the Lord gave him a vision of a pond in the winter that was frozen over with thick, white ice covering it. People were skating on it and having a good time, oblivious to the life in the pond under the ice. The Lord spoke to him and told him he was like the pond with great wealth of gifts and love in him but had not allowed people to share those gifts because he had grown a cold and hard wall around his heart. The Lord told him that many people loved him and wanted to fellowship with him but he was keeping them on the surface of his life.

Jesus explained that He wanted to soften that pastor's heart and break up the ice by the heat of His love, melting the icy fears and intimidation. The Lord said He would do this as the pastor spent time alone with Him, worshipping Him and seeking His face. He also said the pastor would learn new compassion and love for people, releasing to them God's love, joy, peace and kindness. This would also cause him to teach God's Word with new depth of wisdom and truth, encouraging and blessing many.

This story helped me so much because the answer to the healing of his heart was in sitting at the feet of Jesus like Mary in the Bible. Seeking and dwelling in the presence of Jesus is where we are filled, and even saturated with the heat of His awesome love. God's loving presence is the answer to the healing and softening of the hardened heart I know this is true because His love and presence has healed my heart of many wounds.

Forgive Them From Your Heart

It is in His presence that we are finally able to truly forgive from our heart, not just mentally saying, "I forgive them". Forgiveness begins as our choice, we choose to speak words of forgiveness as the Lord taught us, but sometimes the fear and anger caused by that betrayal still needs to be dealt with. The Lord taught me how to forgive through a situation at a place where I worked. We had a supervisor who constantly used hurtful words to several of the employees. One day I was working at the copier and I began to talk to the Lord, saying, "Each day we forgive her and each day she hurts someone else, causing them to be depressed and even go home crying." Suddenly the Lord spoke to me in very clear words. He said, "If you will love her and forgive her and pray for her, I can turn it around."

I had such a moment of complete peace and relief and I immediately began to say, "Lord, I forgive her with Your forgiveness, as You forgave on the cross. I love her with Your love which is unconditional, and I pray for her that You will bless her with all spiritual blessings and that You will heal the hurt in her heart that causes her to act like that." I suddenly had a clear knowledge and understanding that she had been terribly hurt as a child and a great compassionate love from God came for her in my heart.

The Lord then said to me, "Now, take her some flowers." That was something I didn't want to do because she had her favorite person who was always bringing her flowers and we would whisper to her, "Teacher's pet!" We were joking and she laughed, but at the same time we were kind of serious.

I told the Lord I would do that and I got a beautiful vase my sister had given me for Christmas and the lady next door let me have some of her beautiful deep red roses. When I gave them to my supervisor and told her I loved her, she began to cry and hugged me. The room suddenly became like a different place, as though it had been encased in ice and the ice was gone and warmth and love was there instead. It was amazing! This is what God's love, forgiveness and intercessory prayer can do in a troubled situation.

I have found that true and loving intercessory prayer is one the greatest parts of the teaching the Lord gave me concerning forgiveness. Jesus downloaded love and compassion in my heart for her when I prayed earnestly that the Lord would bless and heal her. I have gone through these steps many times over the years and it never fails to work when I kneel at Jesus' feet and ask for His forgiveness of my own wrong attitude. Then I ask for Him to fill me with His loving compassion for the person and I pray that the one who betrayed me would to be forgiven and healed in every area of their lives.

Not only does the Lord fill me with compassion for the person I have forgiven, He fills me with His love for me to the point I can scarcely contain it. There is nothing more wonderful than dwelling in the presence of the Lord and living in His fire of love. That sounds strange I know, but it is the only way I can describe it. This happened to a co-worker of mine when she had been filled with fear, anger and bitterness toward a man who had raped her daughter. She testified against him and this put him in prison, but she told me so many times that he had threatened her and she was afraid he would come after her when he got out. And his time was about up.

One morning the presence of the Lord overwhelmed me and I began to pray for the employees and volunteers at my job, that the Lord would heal and bless their lives. When my friend got to work she was radiant and told us that the presence of the Lord filled her car as she drove to work, so much so that she had to pull off the road because she was weeping so much.

She told us that the Lord had spoken to her during that time and showed her that if she continued to refuse to forgive that man, her refusal to forgive was tying her own hands, tying God's hands to help her, and also tying the perpetrator's hands to ever change his life. She said she actually saw their hands tied in a vision.

When she repented of her bitterness and unforgiveness and began to pray for the man, the Lord filled her and even her car with such loving changed that we scarcely could believe it. And, guess what? When the man got out of prison he never bothered her at all. That is the God we love and serve! That is one way we can know we have truly forgiven, we love them with God's love, even if they transgress against us again and again and never ask for forgiveness. Like parents who truly love their children and continually pray for them, we forgive, no matter what they do.

Whenever I have taught this in a Bible class or in a church service, so many people tell me that this teaching that the Lord gave me has changed their troubled relationships. It has certainly changed my life.

Speak Words of Life

When we speak God's truth from an honest heart, all of heaven and also the devil and his kingdom of darkness will take notice. Heaven rejoices and the devils grit their teeth and go to work to try to bring back the memories of each betrayal so we will open our mouths to speak bitter angry words toward the betrayer and behind their back, instead of words of forgiveness and God's unconditional love. And our words, good or bad, open the door to either God's blessing or the devil's evil works.

I was reading my notes from a Bible class I taught many years ago and this statement from the Lord impacted me now just as it did then; The wonderful secret throughout the Bible for a victorious life is thinking and speaking words of life instead of words of death. We may think we don't speak words of death, but many negative thoughts and words are like a piercing arrow or sword into a person's heart and they never forget it. Those words can influence them and their actions all their lives.

Our lives are shaped by our thoughts and words, and when we speak kind loving words, or cruel hurtful words, to those around us, we shape their lives as well. People produce what they think in their heart and meditate on. It becomes an imagination and then becomes words and they act it out. God made us to be creative beings, like Him. He created the world and everything in it with His words. What are we creating with our words?

And the whole earth was of one language and of one speech.

And they said, go to, let us build us a city and a tower whose top may reach unto heaven, and let us make us a name, lest we be scattered abroad upon the face of the whole earth.

And the LORD came down to see the city and the tower which the children of men builded.

And the LORD said, Behold, the people is one, and they have one language, and this they begin to do, and now nothing will be restrained from them which they have imagined to do.
Go to, let us go down and there confound their language that they may not understand one another's speech.

So the LORD scattered them abroad from thence upon the face of all the earth, and they left off to build the city.

Gen. 11:1, 4-8 (KJV)

This story in the Bible has always fascinated me. I saw a program on TV that taught that the tower was not to worship God but was worshiping the moon and stars and was evil, worshiping the devil. But the thing that fascinated me the most was God's statement that when we are all one and have the same language, nothing will be restrained from us which we have imagined to do. When God says something is true, we can be sure it is true.

For example, we know that people have different love languages. One person's love language can be giving them gifts, and another can be doing something special for them, like doing the dishes or washing their car. My love language is spoken words that encourage and uplift me rather than put me down when I have messed something up. (Not that I would ever mess up! Oh no! Of course not!)

When a man and woman marry, the Bible says they become one.

It is so important that they learn each other's love language. It is built into a man by God to be treated with respect and honor. The Lord has also built into a wife to be loved and cherished tenderly. She may act domineering and tough, but inside she needs tender loving care. Actually, they both need respect and honor and tender loving care, but in different degrees.

> ***As the Scriptures say, "A man leaves his father and mother and is joined to his wife and the two are united into one." This is a great mystery, but it is an illustration of the way Christ and the church are one. So again I say, each man must love his wife as he loves himself, and the wife must respect her husband.***
>
> ***Eph. 5:31-33***

We need to stop and check out our imagination. We think in pictures, so,what are the pictures in our minds about God, and about the people we live or work with? Do we love and respect one another enough to show that love and respect even if we think they don't really deserve it? Can we see ourselves in our imagination giving a gift of love to someone that has just betrayed us and spoken evil about us? It's not always all that easy, but if the Lord tells us to love the unlovely, He will give us the grace to do it. We receive that grace by faith in God. But how do we deal with the emotions of fear and anger that overwhelm us when we are mistreated and abused? Do we fight back or just take it?

Our battle here on earth is a spiritual battle between light and darkness, good and evil. This spiritual battle becomes an earthly battle, a battle for our soul. So, how can we fight and win if it is a spiritual battle to destroy us, spirit, soul and body? The Word of God is the most powerful weapon and it is powerful because each rhema word is a container of God's grace and glory. A rhema word is a specific word from the Lord that you use as a weapon to defeat the devil as you fight the good fight of faith.

Most of the time we are fighting an enemy we can't even see and don't even realize who he is. We may think we are fighting a mean boss or a selfish insensitive mate, when all the time our enemy is the devil who is creating stressful situations and whispering suggestions of fear and blame in our ears.
The devil's favorite trick is to ensnare us with the fear of man. I fought that battle since I was a small child and I have learned that my weapon against darkness is the sword of the Spirit, the Word of God, which truly is Jesus. (see John 1:1-5)

Once when I was working for WAQP TV the host of the show had a word for me from the Lord while we were live on the air. He said the Lord had a wonderful plan for my life and I must keep my focus totally on Him no matter what came against me. He quoted Prov. 3:6 as the one the Lord had given him to tell me:

> ***Trust in the Lord with all your heart, and lean not on your own understanding. In all your ways acknowledge Him and He will direct your paths.***

In studying that verse out, I found that to acknowledge Him means to have an intimate love relationship with Him. That is the key to walking in this life as Jesus walked. He overcame the devil continuously, and He lives in us.

CHAPTER SIX

WE ARE IN A BATTLE

Earlier we talked about standing strong on God's Word when we find ourselves in a spot of trouble. Let's look at Ephesians 6 again in the NLT.

> ***Therefore, put on every piece of God's armor so you will be able to resist the enemy in the time of evil. Then after the battle you will still be standing firm.***
>
> ***Stand your ground, putting on the belt of truth and the body armor of God's righteousness.***
>
> ***For shoes, put on the peace that comes from the Good News so that you will be fully prepared.***
>
> ***In addition to all of these, hold up the shield of faith to stop the fiery arrows of the devil.***
>
> ***Put on salvation as your helmet, and take the sword of the Spirit, which is the Word of God.***
>
> ***Pray in the Spirit at all times and on every occasion. Stay alert and be persistent in your prayers for all believers everywhere.***
>
> ***Ephesians 6:13-18***

I have heard it said by powerful ministers that we must put this armor on every morning as we pray and seek the face of Jesus, even though we have not consciously taken it off at night. I agree because I have had to face people that I believed had an evil spirit driving them and when I stood on special scriptures in the Word of God for each item of the armor of God and deliberately received and applied it, when I faced the person or a situation, I found myself more confident and strong with God's strength to deal with it. However, this cannot be just a religious ritual, it must be an outgrowth of our personal fellowship and relationship with Jesus. He is our armor.

Let me tell you a true story (all my stories are true) that happened to me concerning a demonized person and situation. One day at work someone close to me that I was teaching called and asked me to drive to her city, about an hour away, to help her in a very scary situation. She said she had been playing chess with a Satanist who lived on another floor of the apartment, and for the chess pieces, she played white while he played black pieces. She was supposed to play again that night and she told me that she was suddenly terrified. To her it had just been a game, trying to win him to the Lord and he was trying to win her to the devil. The Lord let her know she was in a dangerous situation and needed my help.

At first my flesh didn't really want to do that because I was tired when I got out of work each night, plus I had received very heartbreaking news just a couple of hours before. I just wanted to go home and soak in a hot tub of water and cry. Tears were just at the back of my eyes and I had to keep them from coming out and running down my cheeks while I was working. I asked the Lord to tell me what I should do, and I believed He wanted me to put aside my feelings and go. He needed me there.

There are situations in each person's life that we never forget because they are such a powerful picture of the grace of God. This is one of those situations for me. I knew I had on the whole armor of God, and as I was driving to that city, I put on worship music that was filled with the Word of God. I sang along with the music, filling my heart with love for the Lord and worship for my King. The whole car was filled with the glory of God as I worshiped Him for Who He is.

When I arrived at her apartment I found the whole room filled with people from her apartment complex who had come to witness the confrontation between good and evil. The Satanist hadn't arrived yet but had sent her a sheet full of questions that he wanted her to answer about God and the Kingdom of Heaven. He said that he had attended church when he was young and had been badly hurt by their hypocrisy and lack of love. He wanted to know if the Bible was real or just a scam to control people and get their money.

There must have been about ten or fifteen people in the room, all carrying Bibles, and I perceived that the room was filled with the presence of the Lord. We prayed and then began to answer his questions by the Word of God. It was so amazing. The man was truly brilliant naturally, but his questions were so basic. As soon as the question was read, the Lord gave me the answer and then everyone would get busy finding the scriptures in the Bible. There was such a joy in the presence of the Lord in that room as we found the answers and wrote them down on the sheet of paper.

The Satanist never showed up. Maybe he was afraid to face all those people carrying Bibles and praying for his salvation. Later I found out that he accepted Jesus as his savior. Praise God! Satan lost that one! One of the best parts of that story involved a little girl, about ten, who came to the apartment looking for her foster mother while we were answering the questions. I saw her come in and at first she stood pressed against the shut door, looking kind of scared.

The lady who was sitting next to me left so the little girl sat in that chair and just silently watched and listened, very tense at first but then began to relax as we laughed and joyously talked about the love of God for that man and studied the Word of God to answer the questions. I remember I turned to her, smiled, patted her knee and said, "Do you know how much Jesus loves you?" She just stared with huge eyes at me, like a fawn about to bolt and run. Then she calmed down and seemed to accept what I said.

After nearly everyone was gone and I was about to leave someone told me that the little girl had been so terribly abused by former foster parents who had claimed to be Christians that now, as a result of the abuse, she hated God. If anyone even mentioned God or Jesus she would act out, screaming and even running out the door and down the street. They were all amazed that she sat there through the whole Bible study and listened and accepted my words to her about Jesus' love for her. I pray that the seed sown that night will bear fruit in her life and she will make Jesus her Lord.

It was late when I finally left and as I drove away I felt a small pebble of sadness go "ploop" in my heart. I thought, "What is that?" Then I remembered the huge boulder of grief that had been in my heart when I left work that day. It was so amazing, I had completely forgotten! I realized that the boulder of sadness was gone and all that was left was the pebble. I laughed out loud and told the pebble to leave in the name of Jesus, that my heart was full of the love, joy and peace of the Holy Spirit, not sadness. It left and I sang with the worship music all the way home, all tiredness gone.

I learned a lesson from all that. Not only had the Satanist received his answers from the Word of God and later on received his salvation, and the little girl finally received the good news that Jesus loved her, I had been healed from my broken heart. What if I had given in to my feelings and gone home and cried in a bathtub of hot water? God's perfect will would not have been done and I would have still had a broken heart. He loves that man and He loves that little girl and He rewarded me with His joy.

Choose to Accept the Assignment!

The Word of God tells us over and over that when we are chosen by God to face a Goliath for someone else, or even for our own lives, Jesus gives us a glorious reward of His joy and shalom peace when we choose to accept the assignment. It may not look like we have won the victory, but the Lord knows that the seed sown will be watered by someone else and the Lord will give the harvest. For example, I didn't know for a long time that the Satanist had accepted the Lord Jesus later. I'm sure the Lord had others sowing seed and watering the seed sown in his life as well.

> ***We just have to overcome our fears and emotions and go forward to obey the Lord, and do it in His strength.***

For sure and for certain the devil will whisper in your ear that you are not capable of winning the battle you face, whether it is small or great. That is when you must face your Goliath and overcome by the blood of the Lamb of God and the word of your testimony. (Rev. 12:11) As we face the giants down and overcome the world the flesh and the devil, we become more and more like Jesus.

Think about it, if Jesus had to face the devil down in the wilderness temptation before He could begin His public ministry, we can be sure we will have our wilderness testing as well. The devil will be right there testing us, looking for our weaknesses and tempting us to give up, saying to us, "Don't even try! You can't do it and you will just fail, again!"

We can recognize his voice speaking to us through thoughts in our mind because his words are the opposite of what the Lord has told us in His Word. Unfortunately we find ourselves agreeing with those thoughts all too often, and then he thinks he has us! He wishes! He hopes we will forget that Jesus is our champion and that He told us He will never leave or forsake us. We just have to believe this in our hearts as well as in our minds. If the devil can get us to meditate on all the times we have failed in the past and the pain of failure and rejection, then he can magnify the fear to the point that we beg God to get someone else for that particular assignment.

I will never forget the story that a famous evangelist told on TV about this very thing. When he was young the Lord called him to a healing ministry, and he knew it. He was so afraid. He knew how persecuted evangelists were who stepped out on God's Word to do the supernatural things Jesus called His followers to do. He told the Lord that he didn't think he could do it and he asked the Lord to please talk with him about it. He kept harassing the Lord to give him some kind of sign or word to let him know for sure he was up to the challenge. So the Lord had mercy on him and opened his spiritual eyes to a very scary and interesting scene right in his bedroom.

He was lying in bed reading when suddenly he saw an evil spirit of death enter his room. He knew it was a spirit of death because it looked just like the pictures of the "grim reaper" with a black robe with the hood pulled over his head. This evil spirit began to choke him and he had to fight with all his might to get the breath to call out to Jesus for help.

Immediately two angels burst into his room, right through the wall. One had a white tunic with a gold belt and the other had a brown tunic with a leather belt. The one with the brown tunic grabbed the evil spirit of death and threw it up against the wall with his huge fist around its neck. The one with the gold belt stood beside the bed studying the evangelist with a puzzled look on his face. The evangelist realized that he was sitting up in bed but the top part of his body was still lying down on the bed. He said the whole situation was so shocking to him that his hair was standing up and he knew his eyes were huge and bugging out.

Suddenly a third angel burst into the room, through the wall again. He said to the angel in the white tunic, "Michael! There's another minister that's in trouble!"

Michael replied, "Alright, take care of him!" While motioning to the evangelist sitting there half out of his body, and was gone out of the room. Now, wouldn't that just freak you out? He said all fear left him about his future because he knew without a shadow of doubt that the angels of the Lord were always on the job watching over us. He was ready to obey the Lord and go to war and we are all called to this spiritual battle.

Stand!

> ***Therefore take up the whole armor of God, that you may be able to withstand in the evil day, and having done all, to stand.***
>
> ***Stand therefore, having girded your waist with truth, having girded your waist with truth, having put on the breastplate of righteousness.***
>
> ***Ephesians 6:13-14 NKJV***

It is so vitally important for our lives that we learn to stand no matter how impossible the situation seems to be. In any war the generals will put the soldiers that are rock stable on the front line because when the enemy comes at them, screaming their war cry, the first impulse built into anyone is to run.

God never tells us to run in terror or cower in fear behind a rock when faced with the Goliath in our lives. And let's face it, just like the story in the Bible of David, we will always have a bear or lion or Goliath to deal with sooner or later. Once we face our giants down, they are easier to deal with the next time. Why is that? Because when we reach up by faith and take hold of God's grace that Jesus paid for, we win the battle. Once we win one battle, our faith grows and we are able to stand confidently in our authority in Christ Jesus for the next battle.

We don't necessarily face a literal giant but we must always recognize when we have to stand for truth and justice, even at the cost of our dignity and even our lives. I'll never forget the time a mother walked down the isle of a packed auditorium and interrupted a famous evangelist's message. She walked in a very determined manner with her arm and finger held straight up in the air and everyone gasped as she marched right up to the evangelist. He laughed about it later, saying, "I always know when someone walks toward me during a service with their finger held high, they are about to interrupt my service." He stopped his message and asked her how he could help her and she told him that her son was going to the electric chair in the next few hours for a crime he didn't commit. The evangelist immediately asked the whole audience to pray and he prayed for the miraculous deliverance of her son.

Later it was announced that the real perpetrator became so agitated and convicted by God that he called the police and turned himself in. The young man was saved. I have never forgotten the love in that mother's heart that would cause her to put aside the natural fear of man and fear of rejection and march down that isle in the sight of thousands of people, standing in faith and courage for her son. Now that is a true David type of courageous stand.

Remember what David said to Goliath just before he ran at him with nothing

> ***Goliath walked out toward David with his shield bearer ahead of him, sneering in contempt at this ruddy faced boy. "Am I a dog", he roared at David, "that you come at me with a stick?" And he cursed David by the names of his gods. "Come over here and I'll give your flesh to the birds and wild animals," Goliath yelled. in his hand but his shepherd's staff and a sling?***
>
> ***David replied to the Philistine, "You come to me with sword, spear, and javelin, but I come to you in the name of the Lord of Heaven's Armies, the God of the armies of Israel, whom you have defied. Today the Lord will conquer you, and I will kill you and cut off your head. And then I will give the dead bodies of your men to the birds***

and wild animals, and the whole world will know that there is a God in Israel. And everyone assembled here will know that the Lord rescues His people, but not with sword and spear. This is the Lord's battle, and He will give you to us!"

1 Samuel 17:41-47

So, how do we stand when we are faced with the awful frightening situations in our lives? We need God's wisdom for that. We must wait for His answer rather than rush in with foolishness and prideful presumption. Get quiet in the secret place of the Most High and worship the Lord in the beauty of holiness. Ask the Lord to give you the answer and then begin to read the Word of God as you stand in His presence.

Hardly ever will we hear a word in a way that seems audible (although I have heard His voice). Usually there comes a knowing in our heart as to the way we should go, and this will always line up with the Word of God. David knew the Lord in a personal way. He knew the Lord's character, that He is faithful and true to His blood covenant with us, and he knew he could trust Him.

What does it truly mean to come against our enemies in the name of the Lord of hosts, or the Lord of the armies of heaven? We know from the Psalms that David wrote that he knew he had a covenant with Almighty God and he had nothing to fear. God is a covenant making God and He will never break covenant. When we find ourselves in trouble, it's not because God took a nap and forgot to watch over His covenant partner. Our enemy is not God, it's the devil, and that's why we need the armor of God to stand in the time of evil.

A final word: Be strong in the Lord and in His mighty power. Put on all of God's armor so that you will be able to stand firm against all

strategies of the devil. For we are not fighting against flesh and blood enemies, but against evil rulers and authorities of the unseen world, against mighty powers in this dark world, and against evil spirits in the heavenly places.

Ephesians 6: 10-12

The Greek word for "stand" is the word *stemi,* which means to "stand upright." Not cringing in fear when Goliath rears his ugly head. I love the story of David because that is the kind of brave and strong character I desire to be. David could stand on the Word of God, not the word of a man, because he knew his God kept covenant. We must seek the face of Jesus and "worship Him in the beauty of holiness," and as we do, He reveals His love and faithfulness to our heart, not just our mind. We must choose to believe His Word and stand for what is right, even in the face of danger and possible defeat.

I heard a true story of a daughter of a mob boss who spent her life trying to hide who she was and what her father did from her friends and teachers. She said she just stuffed the fear and grief into her unconscious mind when there were murders taking place and tried to live a normal life, pretending everything was great.

However, a person can stuff fear just so long and then it starts coming out in one way or another. She began to have panic attacks and started having physical problems, like forgetting how to walk and talk. She had been standing in her own strength and finally realized she desperately needed help.

She cried out to God for help and He began to teach her step by step, how to stand in His strength. She accepted Jesus as her Savior, Lord and King, and as she began to study the Word of

God and to meditate His Word, Jesus downloaded His love and mercy into her heart. One of her favorite verses was Psalm 107:19-21 NKJV.

> ***Then they cried out to the Lord in their trouble, and He saved them out of their distresses.***
>
> ***He sent His Word and healed them, and delivered them from their destructions.***
>
> ***Oh that men would give thanks to the Lord for His goodness, and for His wonderful works to the children of men.***

She stood by faith for her own healing and was able to witness to her father and bring him to Jesus for salvation. It was a step by step process that she received her healing and was made whole. She said she knew this wouldn't have happened if she had not forgiven and loved her father with God's love. She said the dark evil of her environment had been trying to creep into her soul through the open door of fear, caused by trying to hide the evil instead of bringing it to the Lord.

Stand for Others

When we have learned to stand in the face of a giant problem for ourselves, we have the faith to stand beside others who are facing their own giant. My brother, Douglas, will always be my hero and he has stood for me so many times just as I have stood for him. One time he really needed someone to stand beside him in the face of a fire that was sweeping across the area, right toward his property where he was building his house. He only had the foundation and part of the outside walls but the fire threatened to destroy everything.

The fire had swept across the field at the edge of his property and the fire trucks were battling the blaze but firemen advised him to get his motor home off the property because they were afraid they couldn't contain the fire. Several people were watching the fire fight and Doug's pastor was there praying. Suddenly his pastor jumped into his vehicle and took off. Doug was a little startled but he just kept praying and standing by faith for a miracle from God to save his home.

Within minutes the pastor's car whipped into Doug's driveway and he jumped out, pulling a huge cross from the back. Doug realized it was the cross that had been on the wall behind the pulpit of his church. His pastor had ripped it down off the wall and had brought the cross to stand in strong authority against the devil's works.

The pastor strode with great boldness over to Doug's half built wall and slapped the cross down on it, declaring with great faith that Doug's property was protected by his blood covenant with God and the devil had no right to touch it. I don't remember everything the pastor said but God sure heard it and so did the devil. To the amazement of the fire fighters and everyone else, the fire stopped all along Doug's property line. Everyone knew in that moment that they had just witnessed a miracle as the pastor stood on God's Word and faced the devil down with the cross of Jesus Christ.

We must ask the Lord for great boldness and resolve to stand on God's Word no matter how hopeless the situation looks. I heard a missionary tell a true story that perfectly illustrates this. He was on a short-term mission trip to Africa and one evening after service the pastor of the small bush church came running to his tent. He asked the missionary to come pray for a small child that suddenly stopped breathing. The missionary pulled on his clothes and ran with the pastor to the hut where the child lay. He picked the child up and began to pray the Word of God, commanding the devil to get his hands off the child in the Name of Jesus and speaking the Word of God over the child.

The spirit of the child came back into him and he began to breathe. As he went back to his tent, the missionary was praising God for the miracle. No sooner had he gotten back to sleep when the pastor came running back and calling the missionary to come pray for the child because he had died again. He prayed life back into him, standing on God's Word that whatever we ask in Jesus Name the Heavenly Father would do. The spirit came back into the child once more. This spiritual battle went on several times but the missionary never refused to come pray for the child.

The last time the child died the missionary knew he had enough and he held the child up in the air and said, "Devil, if I have to stay here in Africa for the rest of my life to pray this child back to life, I will, so you might as well give it up! Get your hands off him NOW! AND KEEP YOUR HANDS OFF HIM!" That was the last time the child died and was perfectly fine after that. I think that is the resolve we need to stand against the devil and his works by the blood of the Lamb of God and the Word of God, our standard. But how do we become strong like that? I believe the answer is in Paul's prayer for the church in Ephesians 3:14-21

> ***When I think of all this, I fall to my knees and pray to the Father, the Creator of everything in heaven and on earth. I pray that from His***

glorious, unlimited resources He will empower you with inner strength through His Spirit. Then Christ will make His home in your hearts as you trust in Him.

Your roots will grow down into God's love and keep you strong. And may you have the power to understand, as all God's people should, how wide, how long, how high, and how deep His love is. May you experience the love of Christ, though it is too great to understand fully. Then you will be made complete with all the fullness of life and power that comes from God.

Now all glory to God, Who is able, through His mighty power at work within us, to accomplish infinitely more than we might ask or think. Glory to Him in the church and in Christ Jesus through all generations forever and ever!

Amen.

We should pray this Holy Spirit inspired prayer every day and the Lord will fill us with the life and power and love that comes from God. His love will heal every broken heart and set every captive free.

Coming Soon!

Healing a Broken Heart
Part II